Praise for *Written*

T0159838

'A refreshingly honest approach to writing — the authors' upbeat tone will cheer on readers. Writing pros and amateurs alike will be eager to start typing.'
Publisher's Weekly

'The beauty of this book is that it guides you into finding the best writing process for you.'
Forbes

'An invaluable guide to those looking to find new ways to approach their own academic writing and to help others.'
London School of Economics

'This book collects some of the best advice I've ever encountered for constructing a writing habit that actually works.'
Oliver Burkeman, author of *Four Thousand Weeks*

'This book is wise, sympathetic, encouraging and incredibly helpful. It will be a game-changer for so many writers.'
Sophie Hannah, bestselling writer

'An invaluable guidebook for writers at all stages. Evans and Smith understand that process is deeply personal, and they provide a wealth of wise, compassionate advice for breaking unhelpful patterns and creating a flexible, realistic plan for sustainable long-term productivity.'
Mason Currey, author of *Daily Rituals: How Artists Work*

'This is a fascinating and extremely useful book. I recommend it!'
David Quantick, novelist and Emmy Award-winning scriptwriter of *Veep* and *The Thick Of It*

'What a lovely, friendly book. Made me feel cheerful, buoyant, less alone and keen to get on with my writing. Highly recommended.'
Alison Jones, host of The Extraordinary Business Book Club podcast and author of *Exploratory Writing*

'Two things that I love about this book. First, Bec and Chris don't assume that what works for one famous writer will work for you. Their emphasis is on discovering the best way for each writer to get their writing done. And secondly, this isn't just based on hunches – but on extensive study of how writers write. Highly recommended.'
Cathy Rentzenbrink, memoirist and author of *Write It All Down*

'This well-written book on writing well is enormously valuable for anyone wishing to write productively. If you're a writer, first be a reader of this book.'
Robert Cialdini, author of *Influence and Pre-Suasion*

'A fun-to-read and highly informative guide to overcome the most difficult obstacles in writing.'
Gabriele Oettingen, author of *Rethinking Positive Thinking*

"An empowering guide to creating a writing habit that lasts. And a must-read for anyone fascinated by the psychology of performance and mastery.'
Tanya Shadrick, author of *The Cure for Sleep*

'*Written* lays out the challenges that almost every writer faces and provides real-world antidotes to many of the myths and stories we believe about ourselves and why we can't seem to get our projects finished.'
Rennie Saunders, founder and CEO of ShutUp&Write!

'Whatever you write, whatever you struggle with, you'll find real-world solutions here. Warm, wise and practical, it deserves pride of place on your bookshelf.'
Alison Jones, host of The Extraordinary Business Book Club podcast and author of *Exploratory Writing*

'Written isn't just based on hunches – but on extensive study of how writers write. Highly recommended.'
Nigel Warburton, author of *A Little History of Philosophy*

'This is an indispensable addition to the creative bookshelf. It delves deep into blocks, miss-steps and confidence issues, and offers practical and effective coaching. I'll be recommending this to all my students.'
Julia Bell

'If you want to go from "writing" to "written", then you need this book.'
Graham Allcott, founder of Think Productive and author of *How to be a Productivity Ninja*

'The compassion for writers and our strangeness just bubbles off the page.'
Leonie Ross, novelist, short story writer, teacher and editor

'Bec and Chris' course on combatting procrastination is one of our most popular Reedsy Learning courses, so I'm delighted to see they've turned their practical and inspirational advice for writers into a book – it works.'
Ricardo Fayet, co-founder of Reedsy

'I love the breadth and depth of this book – the curated insights into seasoned writers' heads and processes combined with the super practical tips and exercises on what to actually do next. This deserves to be a well-thumbed handbook on every writer's shelf.'
Grace Marshall, author of *Struggle* and *How to be Really Productive*

'There's nothing quite like this book out there. To me, it seems that it might mean the difference between a half-written manuscript abandoned in a drawer and a finished book on the shelf. I know so many writers who will benefit from it – me included.'
Wyl Menmuir, Booker-nominated novelist, writing tutor and author of *The Draw of the Sea*

Written.

How to
keep writing
and build a
habit that
lasts

Bec Evans & Chris Smith

ICON

This edition published in the UK in 2024 by
Icon Books Ltd, Omnibus Business Centre,
39–41 North Road, London N7 9DP email:
info@iconbooks.com
www.iconbooks.com

Sold in the UK, Europe and Asia
by Faber & Faber Ltd,
Bloomsbury House,
74–77 Great Russell Street,
London WC1B 3DA
or their agents

Distributed in the UK,
Europe and Asia
by Grantham Book Services,
Trent Road,
Grantham NG31 7XQ

Distributed in Australia
and New Zealand
by Allen & Unwin Pty Ltd,
PO Box 8500,
83 Alexander Street,
Crows Nest, NSW 2065

Distributed in South Africa
by Jonathan Ball,
Office B4, The District,
41 Sir Lowry Road, Woodstock 7925

Distributed in India
by Penguin Books India,
7th Floor, Infinity Tower – C,
DLF Cyber City,
Gurgaon 122002, Haryana

Distributed in the USA
by Publishers Group West,
1700 Fourth Street,
Berkeley, CA 94710

Distributed in Canada
by Publishers Group Canada,
76 Stafford Street, Unit 300
Toronto, Ontario M6J 2S1

ISBN: 978-1-78578-905-2

Typeset in Garamond Premier Pro by Marie Doherty

Printed and bound in Great Britain
by Clays Ltd, Elcograf S.p.A.

I don't love writing, but I love having written. *

—Jimmy McGovern, screenwriter best known
for creating the hit drama series, *Cracker*

---

* It is worth noting that although McGovern definitely did say this,[1] the same or very similar words have also been attributed, rightly or wrongly, to writers over the decades. Indeed, Quote Investigator reports that the list is long and includes Hedley Donovan, the former editor-in-chief of *Time*; Robert Louis Stevenson, the author of *Treasure Island*; the writers of the 1970s American TV sitcom series, *The Odd Couple*; fantasy author George R.R. Martin; novelist Frank Norris; satirist and essayist Dorothy Parker; actor and playwright Cornelia Otis Skinner; writer and director Sidney Sheldon; activist Gloria Steinem and an unnamed journalist writing for a Louisiana newspaper in 1936. All of which suggests that the words have a certain universality and truth.

CONTENTS

FOREWORD

I've often fantasised about one day becoming a writer. This is a peculiar fantasy, I realise, since by any reasonable definition I already *am* a writer – a newspaper journalist for two decades and the author of three books. But I mean a proper writer: the kind of writer who has uncovered the One True Secret of how to write productively, day after day, preferably in a custom-built writing cabin, at a desk containing nothing but a laptop, a leather-bound notebook and always-fresh coffee in an earthenware cup. To write in such an environment – and here I'm quoting the eternally irritating words attributed to Muriel Spark, about her own creative process – would surely feel like taking dictation from God.

The fact that this book has seized your attention means that you, too, are almost certainly a writer (in the sense that you write things, at least sometimes), who yearns to become a writer (in the sense of finally discovering the blueprint for doing so without struggle, frustration or self-criticism). The bad news is that *Written* doesn't contain the One True Secret of becoming a happy and productive writer, because there isn't one. The good news is that letting go of the fantasy that any such secret exists is the crucial first step to becoming a happier and more productive writer. And this book collects some of the best advice I've ever encountered for dispelling that illusion, then for constructing, in its place, a writing habit that actually works – not for some fantasy version of yourself, or for Muriel Spark or Ernest Hemingway, but for you.

Writers love few things more than dispensing rules for writers; apart from anything else, it's a pleasant distraction from getting words on the page. But fixating on rules such as 'write every day' or 'you need an entirely distraction-free environment in which to write' can easily do more harm than good. They give rise to the belief that you're not a real writer if you fail to follow them. Or maybe you do follow them, for a while, then fall off the wagon and stop writing for months, because resuming that whole perfectly scheduled 'writing life' feels like an insurmountable challenge, when in fact all you needed was to resume a little *writing*.

The truth is that radically different things work for different personalities, different stages of life and different life situations. (In my house, as in many a family home, to be honest, I sometimes need a different approach on Thursdays than on Mondays.) It isn't mandatory to write every day, or in large uninterrupted stretches; I'll even concede – grudgingly, because it's utterly alien to my personality – that even writing in multi-day binges can be the best approach for some. And uniquely, at least in my experience, Bec Evans and Chris Smith offer not a writing system but a system for figuring out your own personal system, tailored to your psychology and circumstances.

Deep down, I think we cling to one-size-fits-all rules because we crave the feeling of control they seem to promise. But in writing, as in everything else, that sort of control is a mirage. Exploring and applying the ideas in this wise, friendly and practical book will leave you with something far more valuable than the fantasy of a perfect writing life. It will help you write much more, and more happily, in the life you're actually living.

Oliver Burkeman
Author, *Four Thousand Weeks*

INTRODUCTION

Productivity is personal

This is going to be perfect, I thought as I stomped through the woods to my new place of work in my box-fresh wellington boots – a thoughtful leaving gift from my ex-colleagues. I'd been hired to run a renowned residential writing centre in rural Yorkshire and I felt like I was beginning a new chapter in my life (pun intended). I loved living in London but the daily grind was, well, grinding me down. Somehow, I'd ended up working in a high-pressure management job which just wasn't me, and it had taken me until my thirties to realise it. My dream was to lead a creative life and dedicate more time to my writing, my long-held passion. I wrote a little in London, but nowhere near as much as I could write if I had more time and less stress in my life – or so I thought.

I swapped my buzzy city office for the tranquillity of Lumb Bank, an 18th-century millowner's residence which once belonged to poet laureate Ted Hughes. Set in twenty acres of steep woodland with breath-taking views to the valley below, the house looks over a Pennine landscape of hills, woodland rivers, packhorse trails and ruins of old textile mills. Today, it's used to host week-long writing courses for Arvon and now, as centre director, I'd be supporting people to write while rubbing shoulders with some of the best authors on the planet. How could I not become a successful writer working here? I mean, hand me a Pulitzer Prize right now. But my perfect plan didn't quite work out.

The move to Yorkshire from London wasn't done on a whim. It was the culmination of years of deliberation. I knew it would come with consequences: I'd miss my friends, my London salary and the security. At the time my husband Chris, co-author of this book, was a freelance consultant and ghost writer. Finding clients wasn't a problem in London, but how easy it would it be in our new home? There were a lot of unknowns. It was risky, but together we agreed that it was worth it; we would be closer to family and could side-step the rat race to fulfil our other goals – like writing.

In my new home I'd have everything I needed to write. More time, less stress, more creative energy and inspiration. But here's the rub: as soon as I started my new job, my own writing ground to a halt. Despite having the ideas, the motivation, the space, the support and the encouragement I needed, I barely wrote a thing. In fact, I had written far, far more when I was living in a tiny flat in London, burned out and working twelve-hour days, than when I moved to Yorkshire and had all the time and inspiration in the world.

Have you ever noticed that when you seek perfection, things rarely turn out as you expect? We often believe we need something else before we get down to the writing. We think we need to find a perfect writing environment or to write just like *that successful writer over there*. All of this may help of course, but what we actually need is quite different.

HOW THE WRITING GETS DONE

Creating anything involves a mixture of craft and practice. To write, you need to be able to spell (at least to an extent) and to understand the rudiments of grammar, style, tone, sentence structure and syntax. Then, depending on what you want to write, you need to grasp the rules of your particular discipline, genre, sub-genre or sub-sub-genre. You might need to learn how to write a three-act structure, plan a literature review, pen a haiku or develop a compelling character. You may need to learn how to present findings, plan a narrative arc or construct an argument. Whatever you write about, there will be certain technical and structural things that you need to know related to your field of writing. All crucial knowledge.

But to write, you need more than to know *how* to write. Knowing your craft is important for sure, but that alone won't get the writing done. At some stage, you have to sit down and *write*. And that brings with it a whole other set of challenges. Challenges that, more often than not, are rooted in the knotty ball of emotions, fears, worries, doubts and hopes that we all have. When you decide you want to write – perhaps why you're reading this book right now – you'll need to find a way to get it written. You will need to:

- find time and prioritise writing over other equally important things
- figure out how to get started
- find a way to continue when you feel stuck, overwhelmed or fed up
- keep focussed: your phone, Netflix, the vacuum cleaner, *literally anything else*, is there to pull you away.

Craft is important, but if you want to write, you'll also need to find a practice that means you turn up and keep going.

● ● ●

When I lived in London, I was incredibly productive with my writing given the time constraints I had. Not that I thought so at the time. Somehow, I was able to churn out short story after short story. Life was busy, but I'd developed a few simple support structures that helped my writing and worked for me. For example, I used to have a long train ride every week, which I'd use for developing my ideas. Nothing too strenuous, just notes, a little creative thinking and some light editing, but I used to look forward to those two or three hours where I could shut myself off from the world.

I was a member of a friendly and supportive writers' group too. We first met at an evening course at a local college and decided to keep meeting up every week in a room above a pub. I also used to stop off to write in the Women's Library on my cycle back from work. It gave me a quiet place to write and was a great way to wind down at the end of a stressful day. In Yorkshire, I had none of that. I had ideas, hopes and ambitions. I had creative inspiration by the bucketload. I used to walk to work every morning with my newly acquired puppy through a sun-dappled forest for Pete's sake – but I'd stopped doing the one thing I wanted to do above all else.

WRITING IS HARD – FOR MOST PEOPLE

People find writing hard for different reasons. What holds you back and what helps you to keep going will be personal to you. I was finding it hard because I hadn't replaced the support structures I'd had in London – in fact, I'd never really realised I'd had any. This meant that I'd started feeling a flutter of fear every time I passed my desk. I can't be the only one who's felt like that. The laptop is set up, the notebook and pen are poised, the space is perfect, I've got the time – so what's the problem? Thinking about it now, the problem was pretty clear. I'd started to compare my meagre efforts to the work of the successful writers I now worked with. My writing routine had gone, and with it my self-confidence. Doubts and fears crept in about my own writing *because* I worked with inspiring and bestselling writers. My grand plan had the reverse effect.

Because most of us were taught the mechanics of writing at an early age, we tend to assume as adults that 'writing' will come easily. But writing – both the craft and the process – is hard. Being good at both is a skill to be learned and developed, just like with anything else. In fact, one research study by psychologists specialising in creative persistence found that there's something inherent about the creative process itself that causes what they call 'disfluency'.[1] Any creative project involves making mistakes, navigating blind corners, getting lost down dead ends, feeling embarrassed by early attempts. All of which makes us more likely to prevaricate, procrastinate, get distracted and quit. Neuroscientists tell us that our brains are hard-wired to crave certainty and avoid risk, but the creative process is the polar opposite of this. Writing inevitably involves trial and error, getting blocked and having breakthroughs as well as randomness and luck. This in turn requires effort, grit, persistence and perseverance. Those things are hard – but it's because they're hard that they also bring such meaning and fulfilment.

It's easy to compare your first draft with the polished outputs of contemporaries or writers who've found success. We can often assume these writers have a natural gift that we don't or that writing must come easily – but is that really the case? Even the most established writers have experienced blocks, barriers and doubts. What they have in common is that they found a way to keep going.

Take Margaret Atwood. In the winter of 1983, she rented a house in freezing North Norfolk in the UK with the intention of writing a novel set in Tudor times. While that novel never arrived, something else emerged instead. Over the time she was there, the plot for the novel she was writing became ever more convoluted, the characters ever more unbelievable and the timeline ever more tangled. For months she struggled to write and spent most of the time avoiding her writing desk entirely by taking long walks and going birdwatching. Maybe it was on one of these walks that she became inspired by the house she was staying in – an old rectory which she says was haunted by nuns. 'Perhaps it was those six months of futile striving ... that caused me to break through some invisible wall,' she writes, 'because right after that I grasped the nettle I had been avoiding and began to write *The Handmaid's Tale.*' As Atwood goes on to advise us: 'Get back on the horse that threw you, as they used to say. They also used to say: you learn as much from failure as you learn from success.'[2]

While six months might seem a lengthy time to struggle with a writing project, writer Mohsin Hamid spent seven years wrestling with his first novel, *Moth Smoke*. Convinced he wanted to tell stories in a way that more intimately involved the reader, but with absolutely no idea how to do this, he figured things out slowly by re-writing the book time and time again from different perspectives. The book went on to become a bestseller in India and Pakistan.[3] Then came the second novel. You might think this was easier to write, but he claims the early drafts were 'terrible'.

Despite this, he kept writing. In fact, it took him another seven years to write his second book, re-writing it countless times until he was happy with the result – or at least, happy-ish. 'My job is to write a book increasingly less badly over time,' he said. But his perseverance led to success: his second novel, *The Reluctant Fundamentalist*, went on to become a worldwide bestseller and the basis for a critically acclaimed film of the same name starring Riz Ahmed, Kiefer Sutherland and Kate Hudson.

Different writers experience blocks in different ways. While some, like Atwood, experience one big block followed by a moment of clarity, other writers struggle with daily doubts and fears. Mystery writer Sue Grafton said that writer's block wasn't a subject she gave much thought to, because it happened to her so frequently.[4] Although the bad writing days far outnumbered the good, the good days were what gave her life purpose. Over the years, Grafton came to think of the blocks she experienced as messages that helped her get the writing done in the long run. Her blocks told her that she was off track. She wrote: 'The "block" is the by-product of a faulty choice I've made. My job is to back up and see if I can pinpoint the fork in the road where I headed in the wrong direction.' She also developed a few tactics to ensure that she could keep going even when she experienced blocks, which included keeping a journal of her writing process for every novel.

If you experience blocks like these, you're not alone. However, how you keep writing through these barriers will be unique to you.

THE PUZZLE OF THE PERFECT WRITING ENVIRONMENT

As Lumb Bank's centre director, I'd say hello every week to a fresh cohort of eager writers. Most of the time, the students would be new, but sometimes I'd welcome returning writers. I'd get to know them and their projects, and over time it would be like greeting old friends. There was one student in particular who prompted a puzzle that stayed with me. 'How's your book coming along?' I asked her one day in passing, as I was clearing up the empty wine glasses after an evening talk. 'Oh,' she said, 'I haven't written anything since I was here last year. I can only write when I'm at Lumb Bank.' Really? Her answer surprised me. This writer had come to depend on the 'perfect' curated and designed structure of a writing retreat. She'd tried countless times to carry on her practice at home but she couldn't do it – things always got in the way.

By thinking about her, I shone the spotlight back on myself. What was it about her life and her psychology that made it impossible for her to get down to writing at home? Why had I stalled, and what was it about my own situation that was affecting me? It also made me wonder what it was about the other writers – particularly the famous names that I hosted to deliver workshops and talks each week – that meant that they could keep going. Were some people doing something right? Was my returning writer doing something wrong? How did they keep going when we had stalled? Did we lack something that they had?

From that moment on (in what I'll admit now sounds like an almighty exercise in procrastination), I started to research and write about other people's writing routines. I dug into the academic research on the psychology of creative practice and persistence. I'd quiz the visiting writing students about their processes, what their fears were, what struggles they encountered, what blocks they had. I also asked questions of the successful, award-winning writers who visited each week. I wanted to know how they got the work done when others couldn't. Was there a secret? These initial investigations taught me that aptitude and talent weren't enough. The writers who were able to keep writing, in good times and bad, had all created successful habits and behaviours that worked for them.

So, joined by my husband Chris, I set up a business to help writers overcome their barriers. A decade on, thousands of writers have been through our courses and coaching programmes. With our help, novelists with writer's block have gone on to be nominated for the Booker Prize, professors have gotten over their barriers and gained promotions, business writers have gained the confidence to write non-fiction books which have turned around their fortunes, and journalists have found the persistence to write award-winning works of reportage.

We conducted research of our own, from in-depth interviews to online quizzes and surveys, partnering with market researchers and academics to explore what stops some people writing and what helps others keep going. In 2018 Chris and I teamed up with researchers and experts from two universities in the USA to run a study into the habits, processes and practices of academic writers – although the findings apply to any type of writer.[5] We surveyed and interviewed nearly 600 authors from around the world, each with varying levels of writing experience, to learn more about how they got their writing done. We wanted to see whether we could spot patterns. When they procrastinated, did they procrastinate in the same way? Did the writers who produced a lot of work use any particular method or tactic? How did the calm and collected writers stay that way? What was it they did (or didn't do) that made the difference? While we couldn't find one common tactic or approach that worked for everyone – there was no magic productivity potion waiting to be discovered – we did find one pivotal thing.

WHY PRODUCTIVITY IS PERSONAL

We found that the writers who were the most productive and fulfilled, least stressed out and better able to cope with the pressures of writing had all built a combination of support structures around themselves – just like I had done in London. These tactics, routines and rituals formed a system that supported them to get started with their writing and to keep going. They were always personal and based around what worked for them in their lives at that very moment. What made these writers productive wasn't one thing but many things, and these things changed as their lives did too.

We expected to find that writers who were older or who had more experience would be significantly more resilient and adept at battling their blocks and barriers, but that wasn't the case at all. We talked to experienced scholars with decades of writing experience who were blocked, miserable and unproductive. Some of these academics had been stuck for years and were on the verge of breaking point – their careers were taking a hit. On the flip side, we also spoke to inexperienced academics at the early stages of their careers who were highly productive and happy. They'd figured out what kept them motivated. It didn't matter to them that they hadn't been writing for long – they tended to ignore the well-meant productivity advice of their supervisors and they just wrote in a way that suited them.

Launched at the London Book Fair in 2019, our research went on to be cited in scholarly articles, quoted in blogs and featured in publications like *Nature*[6] and the *Guardian*.[7] We found that the writers who said they had found specific structures and systems that helped them write were:

- **By far the most productive.** They were the most likely to have written and published the highest number of articles and papers.
- **Better at coping with pressure.** 40 per cent of authors in this group said they feel under no pressure to write whatsoever.
- **More satisfied and happy.** 61 per cent said they were highly satisfied with their writing process.
- **Less likely to experience blocks and barriers.** In fact, they experienced very few.

Unfortunately, we also found that the writers who said they didn't know what tactics worked for them, or who'd never given it much thought, had a tougher time. They were far more likely to be unhappy, stressed-out and anxious. There were also more likely to experience harmful emotional blocks like procrastination, guilt and low-confidence – barriers that can affect mental health and quality of life.

HOW THIS BOOK WILL HELP

One simple idea drives our work: noticing how you write and taking a more mindful, experimental approach to what works for you and what doesn't is the most powerful thing you can do to gain a happier, healthier and more productive relationship with writing.

In our study, the writers who changed their behaviour and built support structures around themselves did so only because they'd noticed what it was that helped and hindered them, and they took action as a result. This mindful approach made them happier and more productive. The writers who wrote in a mindless way – on autopilot – weren't able to change because they'd never paid much attention to their process. Some didn't even think they needed one. This meant that they kept doing the same things again and again – things that didn't work. They were unproductive, frustrated and often unhappy.

Many writing productivity guides and self-help books have a bad reputation. To take thesis writing as an example, one study found a university library groaning with ten shelves of books promising graduates and PhD students the winning formula to academic success.[8] The researchers say that the problem with many of these books is that they take a linear, one-size-fits-all approach that oversimplifies the dissertation-writing process and often makes stressed-out PhD students even more anxious by using scare tactics along the lines of: *if you don't follow this advice, see what will happen!*

This book is very different. As much as we'd love to give you a simple formula to transform your relationship with writing overnight, there isn't one. There's no linear process that suits everyone, no single sure-fire solution that's guaranteed to work for all. But there is a way to build a better relationship with your writing if you take a more intentional approach to your process, noticing what works and what doesn't, and what helps and what hinders. That way, you will find what actually works for you.

This book is the culmination of a decade of exploration and experimentation, as we figured out how to fit writing into our lives and help others do the same. It tells stories about the successes and struggles that writers have experienced throughout history. You'll have heard of some, you won't have heard of others, but their stories will inspire you to pick and choose what might work for your life. It also condenses what we've learned about the brain and writing, through reading hundreds of scholarly articles, books and journals in fields such as neuroscience, psychology and writing studies – so you don't have to! Each chapter considers the kind of questions we know writers want answers to. Questions like these:

- Is it talent or practice that makes the difference?
- How can I tell if I'm procrastinating or just need a break?
- Should I write daily, in small chunks or in binges? Is one way better than another?
- What does a writing 'habit' mean and how do I get one?
- Is it better to dream big or start small?
- How do I keep motivated when I'm not in the mood? Should I push myself – or be more kind?
- If there's no one-size-fits-all solution, how on earth do I find a practice that's right for me?

...and many, many more. Some of these questions might be more relevant to you than others – and that's fine. This book is about helping you figure out what works for you now, but it may be that certain approaches change for you over time as you encounter different challenges. So while it might be tempting to start by picking certain chapter topics and skipping the rest, we'd encourage you to see what you can discover from every section.

At the end of each chapter is what we've called 'The Writer's Sandbox' – practical tips and exercises to help you apply what you've just read. These are the tried-and-tested approaches that we've shared with writers over the years in our webinars, workshops and coaching programmes. Sandboxes are about playing and experimenting in a safe environment, and we hope that as you read this book you see these moments as your opportunity to cast out old ways of thinking and give things a go in a supportive space. We've got you!

● ● ●

How do we know this approach works? Not just because we've helped thousands of people overcome their writing blocks, but because I'm living proof. From feeling stuck in my new home, I found success by learning from others and experimenting with different ideas. Over the years my fresh-from-the-box wellies got worn out and caked in mud, and my London life became a pleasant but distant memory.

My woodland commute to Lumb Bank (often accompanied by Chris and Peggy the Labradoodle) replaced my long train journey as the place to think and chew over ideas. While I didn't have a writing group in Yorkshire like I did in London, I figured out that it wasn't the group as such that kept me going but rather the connection with other people (more on this later on). I realised that 'writing a book' was stressing me out, so I built my confidence by starting small and writing regularly for my own blog. This turned into writing articles for others, which led to a book proposal, an agent, a book deal with a publisher, and in 2020, an award for my first book.

I found my system of approaches by understanding what worked for me at that point in my life. I realised that for me, being a productive writer wasn't about chaining myself to my desk for longer, but rather about working smarter. I found my way to write – and now we're going to find yours.

It starts with breaking some rules.

Part One

THE APPROACH

It is a seductive myth that if we start writing on day one, then we will gradually get better and more confident as time goes on. In my experience this is simply not true because writing is a tug of war between desire and fear, and therefore feels much more like a hazardous zigzagging.

—Cathy Rentzenbrink*

---

* Cathy Rentzenbrink is an acclaimed memoirist whose books include *The Last Act of Love* and *Dear Reader*. In 2021 she published her first novel *Everyone Is Still Alive*. Her book about how to write a memoir is called *Write It All Down*. Rentzenbrink regularly chairs literary events, interviews authors, reviews books and runs creative writing courses.

CHAPTER 1

1

BREAK THE RULES

– because they were written
for someone else

You'd never call writer Cheryl Strayed a shirker. Today, her books regularly hit the bestseller lists and her memoir *Wild* was made into an Oscar-nominated film. She's a successful writer by any measure. But for years she was stuck – she didn't write a thing. She judged herself harshly, thinking she wasn't a 'proper writer'. But one day a thought struck her which changed her life forever.

When you first start writing – or in fact, learn to do anything new – it's normal to emulate other people who have 'made it'. This is what Strayed did and what you might do too. She attended lectures in fancy university halls and readings in bookshops to learn from big-name authors. Sometimes these sessions were inspiring and helpful. According to Strayed, the authors would often share 'secrets' about their writing processes like they were unveiling universal writing rules carved into tablets of stone: 'I write every day. If you don't write every day, you're not a writer,' was an example of the kind of advice Strayed heard.[1]

She, like the other eager fans assembled, would hastily scribble these 'rules' down believing them to be gospel. As an aspiring writer, Strayed took this advice seriously and tried to follow it – but she couldn't. Being the kind of person she was, this made her doubt herself and her own abilities. She longed to write but she couldn't do it like them. Her head must have been full of doubts and fears. But then one day, she had a revelation. She realised she'd been taken in by a myth.

HOW MYTHS SHAPE US

As writers, we often spend a lot of time believing in myths about writing and about ourselves. Sometimes we believe these myths because, just as with Strayed, they've been told to us by people we admire with status and power: other writers, teachers, mentors, supervisors. Often these myths have been shaped over years and are influenced by many different factors: social pressure, our self-esteem, our upbringing and the comparisons we make to the people around us. Over time, the myths crystallise and become ingrained in us, influencing how we behave.

Take Michael Legge, a comedy writer who came to us a little while ago with a problem. He told Chris on their first phone call that he was an 'incurable procrastinator'. This was the myth that had become ingrained in him. He said he lacked focus and determination and that he was at his wits' end because he needed to write for his career. 'Am I not trying hard enough?' he asked. 'Maybe I've just lost it. Perhaps something has switched off inside me,' he said. Legge explained how he would wake up dreading the day ahead. Every morning he'd drag himself to his writing desk and 'try to write'. There he'd sit for hours and hours, forcing the words out. He'd feel disappointed that he hadn't written anything he liked, get distracted by Twitter, feel bad because he'd got distracted by Twitter, do some housework instead, feel bad about that, go out with the dog, sit down again. Chris felt so bad for him as he talked through his guilt-fuelled, gruelling day. Days turned into weeks, and weeks into months. Deadlines and opportunities flew past. And all the while he blamed himself for his inability to 'get down to it'. But then, something big happened. Partway through our coaching programme he emailed to tell us he'd had a revelation about himself and the beliefs that were shaping his behaviour (more on this later) – just like Cheryl Strayed.

Back in her twenties, Strayed wasn't stuck because she lacked talent (her writing record since then proves that) and you could hardly say she lacked determination and perseverance: she is famous for her arduous 1,100-mile solo trek across the Pacific Crest Trail; grit's her thing. But in those early days, Strayed was doubting herself. She was stuck and feeling thoroughly miserable because she was trying and failing to live up to someone else's standards. Her mindset had become fixed and, like Legge, she'd come to believe a certain way of writing would – and should – work for her because it worked for the famous and successful writers she felt she should emulate.

Reflecting on the advice she received in those early readings and lectures, Strayed said: 'You'd look deeper and see that this man – and it normally was a man – would be in his office and his wife would be bringing him lunch. I'd be – "that's just not my life, no one's catering my life". I was bringing lunch to other people. I was a waitress.'[2] Strayed was blocked because she was trying and failing to copy someone else at a different life stage with different priorities, different responsibilities and bags more freedom and privilege than she had at the time.

Strayed was a working-class woman with little money. She didn't have anyone supporting her to develop her craft. She didn't have any high-profile friends or anyone gifting her space to write. She didn't have anyone bringing her lunch. All she had was a low-paid waitressing job, stress, responsibilities and rent to pay. We're not sharing this story about Strayed's first tentative steps into writing to criticise the well-intentioned advice she received. Those writers were undoubtedly gifted and had grit. The advice they gave wasn't universally bad. Daily writing can work well. But it's not universally helpful – and that's the problem. Only when Strayed realised she'd been sold a myth did she change her behaviour. She realised she needed to write in a way that suited her and her life, responsibilities and other work. As we'll find out in Chapter 3, that was to write in infrequent binges of time.

THE 'WRITE DAILY' DOGMA

Why do the myths we believe have such a hold over us? One reason is that they are handed to us as 'truths' by people we trust and admire. One particularly influential voice from the 1980s and 1990s is Professor Robert Boice, a widely respected psychologist who gave the 'write daily' dogma the stamp of scholarly authority after studying academics with writer's block. Boice became so convinced that daily writing was the cure for all writers' productivity problems that his academic papers can sometimes read with the fervour of self-help manuals. Maybe that's why his ideas caught on. He also became very critical of other approaches – binge writing being his particular *bête noire*, something which he linked to depression and other mental health problems.

But while Boice's mantra lay unchallenged for years and became the basis for dozens of books, his work has drawn damning criticism lately from fellow psychologists and writing scholars. One academic, Helen Sword, says that Boice's work lacks rigour.[3] She suggests that followers of Boice's 'write daily' credo base their advice on their own personal experience and therefore believe it to be universal. Daily writing works for them – so they assume it will work for everyone else. Sound familiar? Sword's study of over 1,300 writers found that the writing practices of academics are actually far quirkier and more individualistic. She found no evidence whatsoever that those who write daily are any more productive or successful than those who don't. Perhaps it's no great surprise to find that Boice conducted his research on small groups of senior faculty members at the New York university where he taught.* Scholars with status, privilege and perhaps rather more flexibility, money and time than your average struggling student, burned-out lecturer or jobbing waitress. We believe myths and fall into fixed ways of thinking because we crave clarity and easy answers. We like to know the rules. But while it might feel uncomfortable to think that there is no 'right' or 'wrong' way to write, think of this idea as liberating instead.

THERE ARE MANY WAYS TO GET THE WRITING DONE

If there's one thing a decade of coaching has taught us, it's that the ways writers get down to work, structure their day and keep going are as idiosyncratic as they are. Let's look at a few famous examples.

While you might think that all writers need peace and quiet to work, that's not always the case. Essayist E.B. White could only ever write surrounded by what he called the 'carnival' of family life. His writing room was also the main family living area. He described it as being like the main thoroughfare of the house, serving as a passageway to the cellar, kitchen and a closet room where family members constantly took and received phone calls. 'A girl pushing a carpet sweeper under my typewriter table never annoyed me particularly,' he told the *Paris Review* in 1969.[4]

Some writers are obsessive bingers and only ever write one project at a time. Michael Lewis, the author of non-fiction bestsellers like *Moneyball* and *The Big Short* confesses that his immersive

---

* Referenced in Sword's paper, Boice's 1983 study into academic writing productivity was conducted on just 27 academics.

writing process takes a toll on his personal life. Lewis can only write in intense binges that leave him 'mentally absent for months at a time'. The only way he can work is to pull down the blinds and shut out the world. 'My palms sweat, so my keyboard gets totally wet. Also, my wife says I cackle,' he explains. Lewis laughs to himself and reads out dialogue – and doesn't even know he's doing it. 'I take a lot of time off between books,' he says.[5] Something I bet his wife thanks him for.

Other writers need daily routines and structure. Even when he's travelling or away from home on book tours, writer and artist Austin Kleon keeps up his regular checkbox routine. After breakfasting with the family, he starts work at what he calls his 'analogue desk' (always around 8.30am) and begins by collecting his thoughts in a notebook (always three to five pages) and then jotting down ideas in a diary. Then he turns to his 'digital desk' and writes a blog for an hour or two based on these thoughts. At midday, it's lunch and then a three-mile walk. While the morning is for creating, Kleon devotes the afternoon to what he calls 'selling' – book admin, interviews, marketing and the like. Most days are the same apart from Thursday afternoons which he devotes to his newsletter. 'As long as I write in my diary, publish a blog post, take a walk and read a book, that's been a good day,' he says.[6]

Some writers are tough disciplinarians. Isabel Allende says that January 7th is 'complete hell'. This is because she can only start a book on a specific date of the year – January 8th. Once she starts, she writes every day, getting up at the crack of dawn – including weekends – until the first draft is done.[7] Other writers need a less regimented approach. 'I write when I want to,' Italian novelist Elena Ferrante is reported as saying.[8] She claims not to have any kind of routine and has no fixed schedule either, saying, 'I write continuously and everywhere and at every hour of the day and night.' But she does know that she needs some pressure: 'If I don't feel the urgency to write, there is no proprietary rite that can help me.'[9]

Some writers must plan meticulously before they start. Crime writer Jeffery Deaver spends up to eight months researching and outlining a novel before he writes anything. Some of his outlines can run up to 150 pages long and contain every twist and turn of the plot. He considers writing more of a job than a creative pursuit. Starting by using sticky notes pinned to a notice board, he then gradually moves his visual plan to the computer. Having such a detailed plan means that he never suffers from writer's block – it also makes him speedy. When he starts to write, he can dash off the first draft of a novel in around a month and a half.[10]

HOW MINDSETS ARE FORMED

As coaches, we see writers believing in myths about themselves all the time. When you believe there's just one way to do something, you reject (or fail to consider) other ways, assuming they won't work – this is when they harm us and become what psychologists call 'maladaptive beliefs'. Fixed maladaptive beliefs can limit how we live and the choices we make: they can lead us to pass up opportunities, assume we can't do something, or reach conclusions that can impact the course of our lives.

For example, if you've reached the conclusion that you're the type of person who never finishes any of your writing projects, it often has a funny way of coming true. Your inner critic has a very selective memory and filters out all the occasions where these beliefs were proved wrong. Instead, you notice every time you get distracted or don't finish a project, and conveniently forget the times where you've been able to focus and finish with no problem. We often fall into fixed patterns of thinking about how we should write. If you're certain there's just one way to get the writing done, for example daily in long chunks of time, why bother to try alternative approaches? But in doing so, you close yourself off to different methods and start making decisions based on these beliefs.

Hopefully, reading this book will be a journey of discovery for you. As your coaches, it's our job to help you find out which of the beliefs you hold about yourself are assumptions rather than facts. Let's return to our stuck comedy writer Michael Legge, who came to us with the fixed belief that he was an 'incurable procrastinator'. On our first coaching call he was stressed and anxious. At one point he even despondently said, 'Perhaps I should give up entirely.' But then mid-way through our programme he had a revelation. This is the email he wrote to Chris:

> I've realised I don't procrastinate as much as I think I do. Well, not really. This is what I've learned. Housework is a warm-up for writing. I'm lucky that I have to walk a dog every day. It gets me up and out and moving around. It's basically walking to work. And then, when I get home, I know going straight to my desk isn't quite going to work, so I avoid it. Twitter, Facebook, looking at bargains on Amazon. But my avoiding of work also stretches to laundry, cleaning the kitchen, vacuuming, etc. Before I know it, I've been cleaning, physically moving and thinking for an hour or two and I feel naturally ready to write. I'm definitely getting things done now. I can see my progress. It's not fast, but it's heading in the right direction and it's good. Plus, I have a regularly empty laundry basket.

Isn't that remarkable? Take a moment to think about Legge's message. He hasn't swallowed a magic potion that improved his concentration. He hasn't discovered a secret method that allows him to stay motivated and focussed all of a sudden. He hasn't been cured because there was nothing to cure. His mindset simply changed as he realised the fixed beliefs he held about himself were just myths. Let's break down his beliefs:

- Before, Legge believed that 'proper writers' were able to sit at their desks for hours on end and write. Because he struggled to do this, he thought he wasn't a 'proper writer'. When he realised this was a myth, he started to write in shorter, punchier writing sessions, which in turn made him more productive and happier.
- Before, Legge thought that what he needed was to find more determination and willpower: he thought he should get better at forcing himself to write, concentrate and stay focussed. But the last thing Legge needed was to sit at his desk for longer – what he needed was a change of perspective.
- Before, Legge assumed that activities like dog-walking and house-cleaning were exercises in procrastination and therefore the 'wrong' thing to do. Doing these activities made him feel bad, but a shift in attitude made him realise that these physical activities could be part of a healthy writing process because they helped him warm up and mull over ideas. Thinking of these activities in this way allowed for a kindness that meant he didn't bring any guilt to the writing desk.

Little changed about Legge's actual behaviour, but everything changed about how he believed the writing should be done. By taking time to reflect on his fixed thought and behaviour patterns and then by taking action, he improved his writing productivity, attitude and happiness. Plus, he finished the book he was struggling to write at the time – *Strawberries to Pigs* – and happily, published it in the summer of 2021.

Legge adopted the right mindset. Let's now explore how you can adopt the right mindset too.

●●●

Carol said that she'd had a negative, self-critical mindset 'stamped into' her at about the age of eleven – a revealing choice of words. At that age she was in sixth grade at school in Brooklyn, New York. It was the 1950s and her form teacher, Mrs Wilson, had somewhat traditional ideas about how to motivate young minds. Mrs Wilson thought that IQ was very important – so important that she seated the children around the class in IQ order. High IQ at the front of the room, low at the back. Not only that, Mrs Wilson gave the students with high IQs extra privileges – rewarding them for their 'innate abilities'. Remembering her school days, Carol said: 'If you weren't one of the high IQ students, she wouldn't let you erase the blackboard or wash the erasers, or carry the flag or even have the responsibility of carrying a note to the school principal.'[11]

We don't know where little Carol was in the IQ pecking order, but that's not really the point. According to her, the judgemental school environment gave her daily stomach cramps – I'd be surprised if she was the only one. 'Looking back, I think that glorification of IQ was a pivotal point of my development,' she said. 'Everyone in the class had an all-consuming goal of proving themselves – look smart, don't look dumb. Who cared about enjoying learning when our whole being was at stake every time she gave us a test or called on us in class?'

Later in life, Carol Dweck, world-renowned author of *Mindset* and professor of psychology at Stanford University, realised that by arranging the students in the way that she did, Mrs Wilson was embedding impressionable minds with the idea that their intelligence was something that was set for life. Dweck calls this a 'fixed mindset' – the belief that our qualities, behaviours and talents are unchangeable. Those children labelled as having high IQ must have felt under constant pressure to perform. Those who were labelled as low IQ must have felt stigmatised and hopeless, thinking they could never get any better. Over years of study, Dweck found that our mindsets can have a pivotal impact on how we live.

When your mindset is fixed, it can limit your potential and have a significant, negative impact on your happiness and fulfilment. When you have what Dweck calls a 'growth mindset' and believe 'that your basic qualities are things you can cultivate through your efforts', your life can improve in countless ways.

And the exceptionally good news is that Dweck's research also finds that we are all capable of switching to a growth mindset at any age. 'Although people may differ in every which way – in their initial talents and aptitudes, interests, or temperaments – everyone can change and grow through application and experience.'[12] Often, it's simply a matter of becoming more aware of the mindset you may have fallen into – just like Michael Legge did.

WHAT RULES DO YOU BELIEVE IN?

We always begin a coaching programme by asking a few questions. These questions aren't combative or intended to throw people off balance. We ask them to help people uncover their own mindset: rules that they might believe to be true, but are in fact fixed assumptions based on a myth.

As your coaches, right now, we're not going to tell you that any of the opinions you've reached about yourself or your writing are 'wrong'. We're not going to give you the 'right' solution either. We'd simply like you to examine the things you believe about yourself and your writing and ask yourself whether they are indeed true – or whether they might be assumptions. It's okay if they are. Coaching is about giving you the mental space to reflect on the assumptions you may have reached about yourself. Gentle questions can be powerful and transformational if you respond to them with an open mind. Which is all we ask of you now.

Having read this book so far, what things do you believe about yourself and your writing? Like Michael Legge and Cheryl Strayed, have you reached the opinion that you should be writing in a certain way? Do you blame yourself for not writing for longer or for not being able to 'stick at it'? Have you formed any fixed assumptions about what 'proper writers' are like and how they behave? If you haven't considered this question before, reflect on it now.

When you describe yourself, either internally or to others, how do you do it? What narratives run through your head? For instance:

- *I'm an incurable procrastinator.*
- *I'm the kind of person who can never finish.*
- *I can never concentrate – I'm always getting distracted.*
- *I'm not like [insert name of favourite writer or admired peer], I don't have what it takes.*

Do any of these sound familiar? Has thinking in this way ever stopped you from taking a different course of action or from trying something new? How we respond to life and the actions we take are influenced by the mindset we adopt. When you believe that aspects about yourself are fixed, you take away your agency and capacity for change and improvement.

It's common for writers to experience knock-backs of one kind or another. Perhaps you've received one too. Maybe you've had something rejected, or someone has come back with some negative or critical feedback. This is something that happens to us all, but not everyone responds the same. How would you respond? What would you think? What would you feel as a result? It's normal to want to throw your computer out of the nearest window – you're human after all and nobody likes criticism – but then what would you do or not do as a result? Would you feel hopeless and give in, believing you could never improve (a fixed mindset), or could you instead take the knock-back as an opportunity to learn, develop and change (a growth mindset)?

We're not pretending these are easy thoughts to address. Acknowledging critical or negative self-beliefs can be painful. But doing so means you're at the start of a process to uncover the myths that limit you and the thoughts that harm your writing.

The opinions you may have reached about yourself and your writing are just that – opinions.

The thoughts you have about your abilities are just that – thoughts.

The assumptions you may have reached about how the writing must be done are mere assumptions.

The myths you tell yourself are not necessarily true.

It's time to start afresh and make rules that work for you. Make reading this book your reason to change and take a new and different approach. A healthy, successful writing routine that suits you and your life is possible when you adopt an open mind, believe you can adapt and change – and do one more thing. The next step along your writing journey starts with the simple act of noticing.

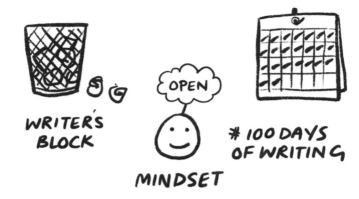

WRITER'S
BLOCK

OPEN

MINDSET

100 DAYS
OF WRITING

CHAPTER 2

TEST

NOTICE

REFLECT

ADAPT

2

MAKE THE RULES

– that work for <u>you</u>

There's *no such thing as writer's block*, thought novelist and creative writing professor Jenn Ashworth – until it happened to her. She was at a crunch point. An award-winning author picked out at a young age by the BBC's *The Culture Show* as one of Britain's best new novelists, Ashworth had written two novels before she turned 21. Now in her thirties, she has published six books, numerous short stories, essays and collections – all to great critical acclaim. Ashworth had written regularly and easily since she was at school, but all of a sudden she was stuck – and it was destroying her.

Every writer gets blocked in a different way. Why this happens can run deep. For Ashworth, a family bereavement forced her to stop writing a project she had been working on for two years. The longer she was away from her book, the harder it was to get started again. Days turned into weeks, until one day she realised she hadn't written a word for over a month and a half. That might not sound like long, but for Ashworth writing is her lifeblood. 'I started to worry that when I opened the file again, the book would be crappy, it would be awful,' she told us. Panic set in. 'I got scared that I wouldn't be able to get back into it,' she said, 'that I'd spent years on it and it was gone, and I'd ruined it. I was really afraid.'

As a teenager Ashworth wrote daily, describing herself as an obsessive diarist.[1] As she became an adult, she balanced writing alongside work and family responsibilities. When it's going well, she feels there's a rhythm to her writing: two days on, two days off, two days on, two days off. 'If I can get it in sync,' she said, 'it works really, really well.' Perhaps it was no coincidence that her block began in the summer, when she wasn't teaching, so she didn't have the routine to her week or much contact with other writers either. Ashworth was alone, lacking structure, lacking support, feeling afraid and grieving.

Unfortunately, we hear stories like this every week. When you care about your writing and it's something you really want or need to do, losing your writing mojo can feel like losing a limb. But you'll be pleased to hear that there's a happy end to Ashworth's story. She overcame her block and is writing again – we'll tell you how she did it later on. But sadly, many writers remain blocked. Their stories don't have such a happy ending – or indeed, an ending at all. Fear gets the better of them; they delay and get stuck in negative cycles. But it doesn't need to be this way. The power to get unblocked is already in you – you just need to know how to find it. This chapter will show you how.

PROCRASTINATION AND WRITER'S BLOCK

The psychologist Robert Boice (see Chapter 1) studied the topic of procrastination in academic writers for years. In his book he links procrastination and 'blocking' in the following way: 'Procrastination has at least two characteristics. It means putting off a difficult, delayable, important task – an act with distant, perhaps doubtful rewards (as in writing) – in favour of something easier, quicker, and less anxiety-provoking (for example, cleaning a desk before writing).' He says that blocking is often similar: 'It occurs when we stumble, delay, and panic in response to a demanding responsibility, when we avoid the threatening task by way of nervous slowing of activity, self-conscious narrowing of scope, even immobilisation. Blocking typically occurs when we face public scrutiny (as in a writing block).'[2]

We're all guilty of kicking the can down the road on a writing project. We pushed the pause button on the book you're reading right now many times for different reasons – some more serious and debilitating than others: work commitments, COVID-19, because the original title was unpopular, because of a death in the family – the list goes on. At various points we've felt lost, overwhelmed and completely unable to write and edit. One way or another, we came out the other side.

But while we stumbled for a few weeks, some procrastinate on an epic scale. Some busy themselves with literally anything else other than the project they should be writing. Let's consider the case of Victorian naturalist Charles Darwin. He only ever divulged his secret theory of natural selection to a few close confidants, telling his friend Joseph Hooker in 1844 that his thoughts on species change felt like 'confessing a murder'.[3] His ideas were first developed during an 1838 field trip to the Galapagos Islands, but he then took a further twenty years to write and publish them in what became *On the Origin of Species*. He might have never published his findings at all if it were not for fellow naturalist Alfred Russel Wallace sending him a draft of his research to review – the exact same theory he was planning to publish. That would spur even the most stubborn Victorian to hurry up and finish.

In the years between coming up with the idea for natural selection and telling the world about it, Darwin kept himself extremely busy – perhaps too busy. He became a world-renowned expert on barnacles. He got really, really interested in earthworms. He studied South American geology, coral reefs, birds and flowers. He even edited a gardening magazine.

We can't say for certain that Darwin's delay was procrastination (he probably didn't know either), but we do know that he feared the consequences of publication. He knew he was on to something controversial that would challenge religious orthodoxy and change the course of scientific thought for ever. That's got to make anyone feel overwhelmed. He was also said to have suffered from very poor health for over 40 years with symptoms like malaise, tremors, headaches, exhaustion and severe tiredness. Don't these symptoms sound to you what we'd call anxiety, stress and depression today? Perhaps confessing 'the murder' weighed heavy in his heart.

In the only recorded interview Harper Lee ever gave about her Pulitzer Prize-winning debut novel *To Kill a Mockingbird*, she hinted at being utterly overwhelmed by its success and the critical acclaim the work garnered across the world.[4] Feelings that no doubt left her wondering how on earth she was going to top the novel's success. 'I never expected the book would sell in the first place,' she confessed to WQXR radio host Roy Newquist in 1964, four years after the book was published. 'I was hoping for a quick and merciful death at the hands of reviewers. I hoped for a little [public encouragement] but I got rather a whole lot, and in some ways this was just about as frightening as the quick, merciful death I'd expected.' While later in the interview she goes on to describe how hard she works and claims that she can become so immersed in her writing that she can spend days inside typing, she didn't publish anything new for the rest of her life. While a second novel, *Go Set a Watchman*, was released when Lee was 89 and in ailing health, there is debate as to whether it was actually just a first draft of *To Kill a Mockingbird* repackaged and sold by her estate without her knowledge or permission.[5]

Lee kept herself busy in the intervening years by starting and scrapping countless projects. Working eight-hour days, she'd write long into the night fuelled by coffee and perhaps a little too much liquor. One meticulously researched true crime book called *The Reverend*, based on the life of Willie Maxwell, a rural preacher accused of murdering five members of his own family in the 1970s, was binned after a decade's work – she never explained why.[6] One reason could be that she only ever had one thing on her to-do list: 'write a book', presumably one which must be at least as good as her multi-million-selling debut novel. Perhaps the most intimidating to-do list of all time.

● ● ●

Everybody's writing blocks and barriers are different. Sometimes we know what's stopping us, while other times the blocks are unknown. Jenn Ashworth was worried that she'd never write again – she thought something had switched off inside her and feared that part of her life may be over. A scary prospect when your writing *is* your life and you define yourself as a writer. But none of these barriers are insurmountable if you take the right approach – which Ashworth did.

In our experience, there's one thing that all people do who manage to successfully beat their writing blocks – either on their own or with help – and there's one thing they don't do too.

The thing they do is to recognise that they're blocked. This might sound an obvious point to make, but admitting to yourself that you are stuck (rather than, say, just very busy) is the first step in overcoming it. Ashworth spotted that she was falling into a negative, unhelpful pattern of thinking and that she was feeling intimidated and overwhelmed by the thought of going back to the book. She realised that the more she avoided the novel, the greater her fears and negativity were becoming. This realisation was important because it made her think differently and question how she could get out of the rut she'd fallen into.

The thing they don't do is to 'try harder'. And by this we mean they don't rely on willpower alone to sit grim-faced at their desk attempting to grind out some more words. And they don't carry on using the same approach that isn't working for them – instead, they change and adapt. Ashworth didn't buckle down or punish herself. She didn't try to 'fight her fears' – she knew that wouldn't work for her. She knew she had to be kind to herself, dial down the pressure, and make the writing feel less intimidating than it was. What Ashworth tried was a gentle experiment to get her back on track, which she started on 'a whim'.

A GENTLE APPROACH TO WRITING PRODUCTIVITY

In order to get out of her writing rut, Ashworth started small. She created something called '100 Days of Writing' and posted the idea on Instagram with the hashtag #100daysofwriting. 'Every day for 100 Days I'd turn up to the book,' she told us. She didn't put herself under any obligation to write for a specific amount of time; there was no goal, no target to aim for. She just turned up – whatever she was doing – with the hope of rekindling her friendship with the book in 100 Days. 'I just wanted to get over my terror. I put this up on Instagram, kind of as a way of holding myself accountable. I thought if I sent it in public, then I'll have to do it.'

Soon, other people were following the hashtag, liking and commenting on Ashworth's posts and joining in. People worked on all sorts of projects, from keeping journals to writing essays, starting novels or finishing their work in progress. The community shared their process and journey on social media.

They all understood the principle of not making it into a hard-nosed challenge but rather a chilled-out, low-stress way of turning up and being accountable to the work. Ashworth believes the gentle approach was part of the appeal: 100 Days of Writing was all about the process. At that point, the output didn't matter.

She turned up to the book every day for 100 Days – sometimes she did very little, sometimes she did a lot. She wrote at home, at work, on trains, in hotels, at a wedding, on the beach, and on holiday with her family. Sometimes she wrote, other times she edited, tinkered and planned, and sometimes she got distracted and procrastinated. It all contributed. 'I spent about 20 minutes just tinkering, and I counted that, and if I was just making notes on a bit of scrap paper, I counted that. It was very up and down.' The key thing is that Ashworth didn't put pressure on herself and kept the stakes low.

By turning up and recording what she did, she also learnt a huge amount about her own writing. 'It was about seeing what it was like every day and trying to observe the process more than the product. I guess, trying to learn why I was so afraid, what worked well for me, and what didn't, which times of day worked and which didn't, and how much could I get done, and just consciously observe all of that and figure something out.'

● ● ●

We love the story that psychologist Ellen J. Langer tells in one of her books.[7] It's about how mindlessness innocently happens over time – it's a nice three-generational tale that might strike a chord.

One day, a woman was about to cook a roast. Before putting it in the pot, she cut off a small slice. When asked why she did this she paused, became a little embarrassed, and said she did it because her mother had always done the same thing when she cooked a roast. Her own curiosity aroused, she telephoned her mother to ask why she always cut off a slice before cooking her roast. The mother's answer was the same. 'Because that's the way my own mother did it.' Finally, in need of a more helpful answer, she asked her grandmother why she always cut off a little slice before cooking a roast. Without hesitating, her grandmother replied, 'because that's the only way it would fit into my pot.'

Langer defines mindfulness as 'the process of actively noticing new things'. Her 40-plus years of experimentation and research proves that being more mindful and noticing how you do things, the assumptions you have about yourself, the myths you tell yourself, what you might take for granted, and so on, is one of the most powerful things you can do to improve your life. She goes on to say that when you live your life in a more mindful way, 'it puts you in the present. It makes you more sensitive to context and perspective. It's the essence of engagement. And it's energy-begetting, not energy-consuming.'[8]

Her research reveals that when you approach life on autopilot in a mindless way – doing the same things you've always done in the same way you've always done them, never taking stock, never questioning and never reflecting – this can have a dramatic negative impact on just about every aspect of your life: health, happiness, relationships, work, creativity – you name it. Over countless studies, her research finds that when you simply pay attention to what you do, how you live, work and interact with others, it can deliver huge benefits.

PROCESS, NOT OUTCOME

As we mentioned in the Introduction, it's easy to compare your early drafts with someone else's finished work. Bec learned this the hard way. She was writing a novel when she first joined the writing centre in Yorkshire. There, she introduced writers like Booker Prize-winning novelist Bernardine Evaristo, BAFTA-winning screenwriter Paul Abbott, Children's Laureate Malorie Blackman and Poet Laureate Simon Armitage. She gushed to the assembled audience about these great writers' talent, their genius and their beautifully crafted words, applauded when they read out passages from their books and poems. But all the while she was dying a little inside. She had so much respect and admiration for these writers and it made her feel like a fraud, triggering her writing block. She now realises that she was falling into the same trap many writers do: comparing her first attempts with their finished products.

Key to the success of Ashworth's approach was that she focussed on the process of writing, not the outcome. The dailiness of that practice, she said, 'lowers the stakes and allows you to be who you are each day'. Compared to the 'write daily' dogma discussed in Chapter 1, which carries with it the weight of needing to produce meaningful amounts of work every day, Ashworth's approach was low-key and therefore very powerful but in a gentle way. Let's unpack what Ashworth was doing with her 100 Days of Writing.

- By having a focus on her process rather than the polished end result, she lowered the stakes – the writing was less threatening.
- By showing up each day, she experimented with how, where and what she wrote.
- By noticing and sharing her writing process on Instagram, she learned about her process in a deliberate way.
- By writing alongside a supportive community, she made the whole process more enjoyable.

Doing all this together, Ashworth dodged the fear centres in her brain which were making her doubt herself and avoid writing. At the same time, the daily small wins stimulated the reward centres of her brain, which in turn built her motivation and made her want to come back the next day, and the next.

'The definition of insanity,' someone other than Einstein famously said, 'is doing the same thing over and over again and expecting a different result.'[9] Strict writing routines can work for some people, but for others it can mean we fall into writing ruts and start to believe negative things about our writing ability. When you realise, as Ashworth did, that writing can be done in many different ways, this impacts your mindset and ultimately your behaviour. Sometimes you just need to try something different.

IT'S TIME TO MAKE YOUR OWN RULES

After spending thousands of hours coaching writers to write, we have found that noticing things about your process is the single most powerful thing that you can do. When you take a record of how you write – something we'll show you how to do – and make an honest appraisal of your thoughts and assumptions, you start to spot patterns in your thinking and your behaviour. It's only by spotting these patterns – the good and the bad – that you can uncover what works for you and what doesn't.

If noticing or being more mindful sounds a bit wishy-washy to you, think of it as a process of personal data gathering. A researcher would never reach a conclusion based on a set of assumptions – they'd ground it in evidence. All you're doing with a more mindful approach is building up a dataset so your beliefs about yourself are based in fact – not assumption and myth. That is why Ashworth's 100 Days of Writing was so effective: with the sole intention of showing up each day and sharing her process, she gathered a huge amount of data. Five years on from her first 100 Days, we asked her what she's learned.

She started by telling us that bad things are always going to happen. 'It's not every year that someone close in your family dies, but every day something happens to get in the way of the writing. It is possible to turn up and be a writer and have all that normal stuff happen in your life.' While the first 100 Days was all about gentleness, the others have been different. For example, in 2019, she had a burning idea that just needed to be written – the 100 Days of Writing became a container for her 'exuberance'. She ended up writing a complete novel in that attempt, something which was very unusual for her. When the COVID-19 pandemic hit in 2020 it was quite the opposite – she had to abandon writing partway through to homeschool. Again it all comes down to noticing: 'knowing when you are beat. Like, there's a global pandemic on, sit down, watch telly, shut up. That was really what I needed.' Her 100 Days in 2021 were about community, extending the invitation to others so together they could explore what it meant to turn up to the page each day, to share on Instagram and write together on Zoom each Sunday.

NOTICING IS YOUR SUPERPOWER

Noticing can be simple and shouldn't require much effort. Don't think of it as *another thing I have to do* – all it involves is a moment of reflection after each writing session. Try to ask yourself these three questions:

- What went well?
- What didn't go so well?
- What will I do differently next time?

Log your observations in a notebook, type them into an Excel sheet, voice note your thoughts on your phone – whatever works for you. The main thing is to have a record so you can start to spot patterns in your thoughts and behaviour. At the beginning it might feel odd. You might wonder what the point is – but stick with it. We promise that after a few short days you'll spot insights that will be transformative. Make sure to note these insights as well. This is not an opportunity for you to beat yourself up or feel guilty. Instead, notice things as a scientist might observe things in a lab – without judgement. Here are five ideas that might trigger some insights for you.

1. Do you write better/worse on certain days of the week or times of the day?
2. When you find writing 'hard', what makes it hard?
3. When you've had a 'good' session, what made it good?
4. Are there days when your inner critic is particularly vocal? What is it saying?
5. If you get distracted or feel you're procrastinating, what do you get pulled away by?

Crucially, noticing should lead to action – otherwise it's just navel-gazing. If there are practical things getting in the way, think about how these could be avoided or worked around. If your barriers are more emotional and psychological, note these thought processes down.

All writing is trial and error – little experiments towards an answer of some kind. We love these words from entrepreneur and non-fiction author Margaret Heffernan because they offer such a positive way to look at the writing process: 'The great advantage of experiments is that they stop you from being stuck. They're one way to prototype a future we think we want. You could say that experiments are how we learn everything. We try to stand up, fall over, recalibrate and next time find we can teeter for a second or two. Keep at it and mastery emerges.'[10]

While Ashworth is a celebrated writer and a highly regarded professor of creative writing, she stresses that 100 Days of Writing is not about showing off her expertise but rather an invitation to show up with your writing – whatever you are writing and however you are feeling. 'Some days I can have epiphanies,' she told us, 'that will last my entire life and need to be shared across the nation. And the next day I want to sit in bed and eat Pringles and sulk because it was a crap idea to do this.' She believes that deep down we know what's good for us and what we need to do. Changing your mind and changing your process is part of it. For example, Bec borrowed Ashworth's approach when she wrote her first book. After signing the contract with the publisher, she realised that she had just over 100 days to write and submit 60,000 words. Hers was not a gentle approach, but one that was fast and furious, which suited her life at the time. She got out her planner, allocated 100 days to her writing (allowing for a few days off and a week's holiday) and got going.[11]

Ashworth stresses that there is no one way to write, so what worked for her (and Bec) might not work for you. But in order to find what does work for you, you'll need to start by noticing how you write and trying out different approaches.

How you get the writing done – how you make the time, prioritise your work, keep motivated, avoid procrastination, resist distractions – is personal to you. Other people's ways of working might help – but they might not. Don't ignore the well-meant advice from gurus, supervisors, famous writers, teachers – and so on. We'd encourage you to read widely and drink all this in – but don't think it of it as gospel truth either.

FIND YOUR PERSONAL APPROACH

You might recall that in the Introduction, we talked about how writing can be a hard thing to do because the creative process itself is chock-full of the kind of unknowns, false starts and blind alleyways that our brains dislike. This is something that we know about first-hand, not only from writing but from designing our coaching model over the last ten years – a process of trial and error if ever there was one. When we first started, these programmes were more like lessons. We'd give people tips to get unblocked, keep motivated and so on. These programmes were good, but there was always that niggling feeling that something was missing – but what? The only way we could figure out the missing element was to keep going – keep developing coaching programmes, testing out ideas and getting feedback. This hasn't been easy. It's caused arguments and it's often left us strapped for cash. But then one day, we had a breakthrough.

It's sometimes tempting to skip the first part of a book like this in order to quickly access the juicy tips and advice in the middle, so we'd like to thank you for reading this far. What we hope we've managed to achieve in this first part is to convince you that how you take on board advice and experiment is just as important as what ideas and approaches you test out. This was our aha moment with our coaching model. We'd been giving people advice and tactics (and way too many things to do), but we hadn't been giving them an approach. We'd been telling them what to do, not how to do it.

As you read Part Two and build your personal approach, we'd encourage you to write deliberately and mindfully. In other words, don't write on autopilot! Be aware of which tactics work for you and which don't. Gather data. Adapt as a result and be open about changing. Think about what myths might have seeped into your psyche. Do you have any preconceptions about what the 'right' and 'wrong' ways to write are? If so, set these to one side for now. Be ready to experiment and play – learn things about yourself as you go. Some things will work, some things won't. Test out ideas – use ones that work, discard ones that don't.

This model might help:

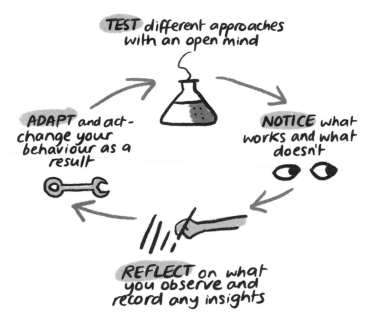

Earlier we wrote about psychologist Ellen J. Langer's work on mindfulness. Let's return to her again for some words that can guide you as you write: 'The rules you were given were the rules that worked for the person who created them, and the more different you are from that person, the worse they're going to work for you. When you're mindful, rules, routines and goals guide you; they don't govern you.'[12]

Consider reading this book your opportunity to question the assumptions you may have reached about your writing. This is your chance to push the reset button and do things differently – take it without fear. You know how to notice and take a more mindful approach to your writing. You understand the power of doing so with an open mindset. Now let's get to work.

Part Two

START WRITING

I bribed myself with the future. I dangled the things I wanted in front of my greedy eyes, and in the flush of that desire I reminded myself that writing five hundred words right now *would reel in the world I wanted. There is always something you can do right now; there is always a first step, no matter how small it is.*

—Akwaeke Emezi[*]

---

[*] Akwaeke Emezi is a Nigerian-born video artist and multi-award-winning fiction writer best known for their novels *Freshwater, Pet, You Made a Fool of Death With Your Beauty* and their *New York Times* bestselling novel *The Death of Vivek Oji*. Their astounding memoir *Dear Senthuran* explores how to carve out a future for oneself as a writer.

SPONTANEOUS

SAME TIME   SAME PLACE

DAILY

CHAPTER 3

TIME BOXING

BINGE

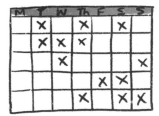

3

TIME

*Plan and prepare for your writing time,
however infrequent it may be*

It was Monday morning and Graham Allcott was doing a weekly review of his to-do list. For the last year, one item had made very little progress: 'write book'. Like many of us, he had ambitions to write. He knew there was a growing audience for his ideas and a demand for the lessons he'd learned after setting up his business. However, he had barely scratched the surface of an 80,000 word target. 'I began to realise,' he said, 'that the reason it wasn't moving forward was because books require a lot of headspace and focus. And running a business, I was too engrossed in the day-to-day to create that space.'[1]

Allcott isn't just any wannabe author. He's the original Productivity Ninja, the founder of Think Productive, a business that helps companies around the world transform how they get work done. Yet, here he was, unable to write his book because he was too busy helping other people up their productivity – oh the irony. Lack of time is a problem many writers have. We know because in 2014 we asked over 500 writers what holds them back the most, and 'lack of time' came top.[2] Thankfully, Allcott found a solution (it might have been a bit embarrassing if he hadn't) and that was to get someone to run his business while he went away to write.[3] 'My answer was a little drastic but it worked,' said Allcott.

'I spent a month living in a beach hut in Sri Lanka, empowered by home-cooked Sri Lankan food, a wifi-free stretch of coastline, stunning views and the knowledge there was nothing else to do but to use this space I'd created to create. The full draft was done a month later.'

The 'grand gesture' approach comes up a lot when you study the habits of writers, creatives and workers tackling ambitious or long-term goals. These grand gestures can take many different forms, from quitting jobs to hunkering down in writing huts, taking sabbaticals or going on retreats. Author Cal Newport extols the value of grand gestures in his book *Deep Work*, insisting that they are driven by the psychology of committing seriously to the task at hand. He explains that putting yourself in an exotic location, taking a week off from work, or locking yourself in a hotel room. 'These gestures push your goal to a level of mental priority that helps unlock the needed mental resources. Sometimes to go deep, you must first go big.'[4]

Before you fling this book across the room in fury, we are not suggesting that jetting off to a desert island is a realistic solution for many of us. However, when we surveyed over 3,500 writers on how they fit writing into their lives, it was one of the four approaches that emerged (we'll go into each one in detail soon):[5]

1. **Spontaneous writing** is used by people who have unpredictable or packed calendars.
2. **Daily writing**, often at the same time and place, is an approach beloved by productivity gurus and masters of habit.
3. **Binge writing** involves rare but deeply productive writing sessions such as on a retreat or sabbatical (or a hut in Sri Lanka, in Allcott's case).

4. **Time boxing** is a practical approach to scheduling writing time around the rest of life's demands.

Allcott called his approach drastic, but in truth it's very pragmatic. The book was a long-term goal that was central to his business, so his solution had to be big, bold and brave – otherwise the book simply wasn't going to get written.[6] These kinds of grand gestures aren't always possible of course, but Allcott encourages writers to still make space for what matters: 'My Sri Lanka when I did the next book,' he said, 'was our spare room with our six-month-old child crying in the next room, but it was beautiful because I could spend time with him.'

NO TIME TO WRITE?
'I mean, none of us anymore have long leisurely uninterrupted days to write,' said Cynthia Selfe.[7] A distinguished humanities professor emerita at Ohio State University, Selfe was an early champion in the field of computers and writing: she was the first woman and first English teacher to receive the prestigious EDUCOM Medal for her use of computers in higher education. She's a prolific writer too, having written five books, ten edited collections and nearly a hundred papers. Yet she has very limited time to write – so how does she do it?

Her solution is the polar opposite of Allcott's grand gesture. She writes around her other tasks in what she calls 'small little moments of the day'. These can be ten minutes, five minutes, or even just two minutes. She finds the time in between a student conference and a committee meeting, in between a class that she's teaching and her yoga exercise. She likes to write when she's doing other things like watching TV, or during faculty meetings when she tackles essential writing admin such as indexing or mindless tasks that are small enough to pay attention to at the same time. Selfe said: 'There's all these demands in our day, so if I can't use these small times or interstices of my day, then projects don't get done.'

You might not think that all those scrappy bits of time in your day would add up to much – but they can. Author Brigid Schulte, a working mother of two, thought she had no time to write, but when she took part in a time-use study, she discovered she had a whacking great 27 hours available each week. However, this available time was fragmented and interrupted by temper tantrums and daily domestic duties. Schulte coined the phrase 'time confetti' to describe the 'bits and scraps of garbagey time. Five minutes here. Ten minutes there. Listening to the radio, exhausted, trying to get out of bed. Getting some exercise. Waiting by the side of the road for a tow truck.'[8]

Don't think of this as highly productive time when creativity is seeping from every pore. If you're spending a few minutes looking at your project while your car tyre is being changed, you're not going to bring your writing A-game, but you might be able to do a little. With four out of five* adults feeling that they have too much to do and not enough time to do it, researchers have found that people who *feel* time-poor experience less joy each day; they laugh less, they are less healthy, less productive, and more likely to divorce.[9] One of the solutions offered for escaping these time traps is to make better use of what time we have. That's exactly what one group of writers we studied did.

---

* In our own survey of writers, we identified around 11 per cent had an abundance of time to write. While this might seem like a gift, writers with no structure are often the biggest procrastinators, finding literally anything else to do rather than write. If this is you, you'll find our advice on managing distractions in Chapter 6.

1. Spontaneous writing

Our research found that some people are so busy from dawn to dusk, or have such chaotic and unpredictable days, that the only way they can write is to do so in a spontaneous way.[10] When you write spontaneously, you're ready to write at the drop of a hat. Writers who use this method become attuned to using any opportunity to write, making the most of delayed trains, cancelled meetings and sleeping children. Like Selfe, they are not impulsive or inspiration-driven, just incredibly prepared. We'll help you to get organised with exercises at the end of this chapter.

This approach has been studied in academic writers – not an area you'd think would lend itself to a spontaneous approach. However, according to Christine Tulley, the author of *How Writing Faculty Write*, it can. Her goal was to create a *Paris Review* for scholarly writing, and her book of interviews explores the habits and strategies of what she calls 'rock stars' in the field of writing studies – people who write about writing, teach writing skills and research writing behaviours. She found the writing strategies these scholars have developed over time were born of necessity. Take the technique of 'toggling' between tasks. We asked her what this looked like for the time-starved academics she interviewed. 'If they have just five or ten minutes before a phone call or have to attend a meeting,' Tulley said, 'they immediately switch over to their writing. Instead of filling the time by checking email or doing an admin task, these writers prioritise their writing – over everything else.'[11]

This approach runs contrary to much of the advice on how to be productive. Many writing guides advocate daily writing sessions of an hour or two to optimise attention. Tulley admits that it's unlikely that any deep, concentrated work gets done in those times, but writers are able to do something that moves their project on, like checking through a paragraph or making a tweak here and there. 'Having regular contact with their project over the day means they don't lose momentum with it,' she said. In fact, having pockets of time can be more helpful than having longer scheduled writing time. She says: 'One writer told me it works for them because the pockets of time are so small. Because it's just ten minutes, nobody is trying to steal it from you. Once you get to the point where you have 30 minutes free, someone will want to take it.'

In short, spontaneous writing is driven by necessity and circumstance rather than being designed for serious concentration and creative flow. Some people just can't dedicate a complete hour for a writing session, so they have to rely on time confetti. We found that the writers who used this approach often wrote for an hour or more a day even though it was scattered into five-, ten- or fifteen-minute mini-sessions. There are downsides, such as writers struggling to step back and consider the bigger picture for tasks where a more strategic overview is required. Also, working on a large project would take significant persistence to finish. However, the repeated contact with their work in progress meant that new ideas emerged as writers mulled over their writing between sessions; they also learned to restart quickly and avoid procrastination. So, while this might not be the most efficient way to write, spontaneity is a valuable tool that helps writers make use of whatever moments present themselves.

2. Daily writing

In *An Autobiography*, Anthony Trollope surveys his life with much satisfaction: 'I feel confident that in amount no writer contributed so much during that time to English literature.'[12] While not afraid to blow his own trumpet, Trollope did indeed have an output that is remarkable. As well as the publication of more than 60 books, his list of achievements included his critical, social and sporting articles, the work he did for the General Post Office (famously introducing the beloved red postbox to Great Britain), twice-weekly fox hunting (well, he was born in 1815), playing whist at the Garrick Club, socialising at home, and at least six weeks of foreign holidays a year. He concludes: 'Few men I think ever lived a fuller life and I attribute the power of doing this to the virtue of my early hours.'

Trollope had the ultimate morning ritual, writing every morning before work, aided by his 'old groom'* who was paid to wake him and bring him coffee. He says: 'It was my practice to be at my table every morning at 5.30 A.M.; and it was also my practice to allow myself no mercy. By beginning at that hour I could complete my literary work before I dressed for breakfast.'†

Daily writers, who work habitually at the same time and place, are often considered to have the gold standard in writing productivity.[13] One research project we ran found that daily writers report feeling happier with their writing (though perhaps not to Trollope-levels of satisfaction), perhaps because they are in constant touch with it in a predictable way.[14] The regular routine offers comfort and takes away the struggle with willpower and finding time.

Trollope believed that literary labourers who write daily should be trained to write continuously – it was not for him to 'sit nibbling his pen, and gazing at the wall before him, till he shall have found the words with which he wants to express his ideas'.[15] Much like spontaneous writing, there is little time to procrastinate when you write daily. There is much to emulate in Trollope's approach.

---

* Aided by money and privilege.

† While we're sure Trollope wrote in a beautifully tailored writing jacket, this quote always makes us giggle as we imagine him writing naked before he got dressed. Either way, we salute whatever choice of writing attire helps get the words down.

Before we start comparing ourselves to his output (and generous holiday allowance) the part of his approach we're interested in is his 'noticing'. As we've seen in the previous chapter, when you start to pay attention in a more mindful way to how you get the writing done (or not done), then you can change. Trollope used a journal to log his writing, focussing specifically on output. He explains:

> When I have commenced a new book, I have always prepared a diary, divided into weeks, and carried for the period which I have allowed myself for the completion of the work. In this I have entered, day by day, the number of pages I have written, so that if at any time I have slipped into idleness for a day or two, the record of that idleness has been there, staring me in the face, and demanding of me increased labour, the deficiency might be supplied.

Being the kind of meticulous, Type-A personality that he was, Trollope measured his output against goals, which he was very precise about. He aimed for a target number of pages a week, and because words have a 'tendency to straggle' he calculated that a page contained 250 words. Across his career he averaged 40 pages per week, which varied from a self-proclaimed 'low' of 20 pages to a high of 112 pages per week. We could be flabbergasted at his envy-making peak of 28,000 weekly words, but let's look instead at the variation from his 'low' of 5,000 words per week. Even the master of routine had good days and bad days – this is similar for other daily writers we've spoken to. By showing up each day, they are better able to weather the peaks and troughs of writing – if they have a bad day, they simply turn up tomorrow, the day after and the day after that, and all of this combines to make consistent progress.

While it's easy to poke fun at Trollope for his pride in completing his work 'exactly' within his proposed dimensions, his satisfaction is counterbalanced with a harsh judgement of himself. He felt it was important to have the journal as the 'record before me, and a week passed with an insufficient number of pages has been a blister to my eye, and a month so disgraced would have been a sorrow to my heart'. So, while noticing how you write and gathering evidence can be helpful, the drawback is that it can all too often lead to negative self-judgement and a sense of failure. Trollope's 'sorrow' provided a spur to action – it took him a lifetime of trial and error to design a routine that enabled him to create around the many and varied activities in his life. He speaks frankly of his failures and of the necessity of having to earn a living elsewhere. His advice to 'young aspirant' writers is to persevere, to try and to fail – in other words, to keep on experimenting, to notice what works and what doesn't, and to adjust your approach based on evidence.

Next we'll look at two more approaches, starting with the most frowned-upon in productivity circles – binge writing.

3. Binge writing

'My name is Cheryl Strayed and I am a binge writer.'[16] You might recall meeting Cheryl Strayed in Chapter 1, who early on in her writing career had fallen for a myth. For many years she judged herself, feeling inadequate that she wasn't a proper writer. Her doubt came from comparison, one of the most toxic forms of self-sabotage available to writers. Strayed would listen to writers offering advice such as: 'If you don't write every day, you are not a writer.'

Remember how Strayed felt pressure to write in the exact same way as the famous writers she wanted to learn from? She wanted to be like Trollope, but instead she was his groom. Starting with the reality of bringing lunch to others rather than the other way around, she designed her own way to write. Her liberating advice on writing, as with everything in life, is that you have to do it in a way that works for you. For her, that meant abandoning the pressure to have a daily writing practice and instead scheduling in what was possible. She starts by identifying when she can't write: 'I do best when I can say that this is the block of time that I'm not going to be able to write. Even if it is a couple of days, sometimes it's a couple of months.' This is an important step as it releases her from any kind of guilt or shame that she should be writing when she's not writing. The next step, what she calls a counterpoint, is to identify when she is going to write and then arrange her life so that happens. She summarises: 'So what that looks like for me is that it's not so much a daily practice, as it's looking at the month and seeing when can I write and when am I not going to write.'[17]

Strayed is a self-proclaimed and unapologetic binge writer, and we only need to look at her output to find evidence that it works. Her version of binge writing has more in common with the grand gesture approach described at the start of the chapter – essentially a retreat from the demands of normal life to focus solely on writing. In her research, admired educationalist and author Rowena Murray explains that retreats are so effective because they both legitimise writing and privilege it over everything else. Murray establishes the principles of a retreat as 'dedicated writing time, without interruptions and without the threat of interruptions, which, for some, is not available either at home or at work. There is also non-surveillance, in the sense that participants' outputs are not measured.'[18] She describes writing retreats not as a 'last resort' but as a way of becoming a more productive writer.

However, the negative narrative around binge writing remains. It all started in the 1980s with a study into procrastination led by psychology professor Robert Boice. It identified procrastinators who wrote in binges, defined as 'hypomanic, euphoric, marathon sessions to meet unrealistic deadlines'.[19] When the procrastinating bingers were compared to those who wrote in brief daily sessions, the conclusions were stark. Bingers:

- ↢ wrote significantly less
- ↢ listed fewer creative ideas for writing
- ↢ got fewer editorial acceptances
- ↢ didn't progress as far in their career
- ↢ scored higher on tests for depression.

The study went on to say that binge writing was counterproductive and potentially a source of depression and writer's block: 'Productive creativity seems to occur more reliably with moderation of work duration and of emotions, not with the fatigue and ensuing depression of binge writing.' So, a pretty damning indictment all round. While long intense sessions might get the words on the page, it comes with a psychological cost that results in fewer creative ideas and mental health problems – at least, according to Boice.

But in reality, this research was a study into procrastination, not binge writing. Doing anything will stress you out if you don't leave enough time for it, wait until the last minute and do it in a blind panic. But binge writing doesn't have to be like this. Strayed shows that it is possible to plan this approach and make a success of it. What if binge writing was scheduled and intentional – would it lead to the same negative outcomes? Our research found that successful binge writers don't write in a deadline-driven panic but instead schedule sessions of uninterrupted deep work – days that are as productive as they are rare.[20] We'd like to see a comparison of planned versus procrastinating binge writers. Granted, there are downsides: binge writers can be prone to raised expectations and perfectionist tendencies because they crave the ideal conditions to write, such as academic writers who plan to write on sabbatical, but it doesn't have to be this way.

Imagine your own Sri Lanka and create a version of a retreat that's available to you – book a babysitter for a full day and go to a local library, or work from a neighbour's kitchen table while they're at work (we suggest getting their permission first). It might require some thought, and some return favours, but it doesn't have to cost money. For Strayed that meant checking into a hotel down the street from her home for two nights. She told her husband not to interrupt her unless 'somebody stops breathing'. Thankfully, everyone kept breathing, she found her flow and wrote more in those 48 hours than she had for weeks at home. Strayed offers advice to people like her who want to write – those with jobs, families, caring commitments, over-busy and over-committed lives, who don't have help to take care of the catering, shopping and admin of the daily grind. She advises making an intention to write – a goal, a target, or just a mindset – and then sticking to it.

'Make an intention and follow through with it. So, if all you can do is write one day a month, say "I'm going to take one day a month that's all I'm doing" – that's twelve good days a year, there's a lot of writing you can get done.'

Once you embrace the reality of your over-committed schedule you can realistically plan to write. Successful binge writing is about being deliberate. Not only is this a super practical way to organise your time, it also squashes any feelings of guilt by acknowledging how little spare time you have.

4. Time boxing

Back in 2008 a PhD student shared the details of his daily schedule.[21] While many of his fellow researchers at the Massachusetts

Institute of Technology followed the 12pm to 3am 'MIT cycle', he was able to stick to a nine-to-five workday with a top-up session on a Sunday morning. He didn't have a lighter workload – quite the opposite: in addition to being a graduate student on a demanding programme, writing his final dissertation alongside several research papers, he was a teaching assistant and a staff writer for a magazine, had a prolific blogging habit, was taking additional courses and also researching material for a book he was writing. That graduate student was Cal Newport (whom we met earlier), digital minimalist, father of the deep work movement, and advocate of a more intentional approach to work-life balance. An approach that prioritises the important things in life – in his case, writing, research and spending time with his family. His secret to balancing an ambitious workload with an ambitiously sparse schedule was an approach called 'fixed-schedule productivity'.

There are two rules for his system:

1. Choose a schedule of work hours that you think provides the ideal balance of effort and relaxation.
2. Do whatever it takes to avoid violating this schedule.

Sounds simple, doesn't it? But it's incredibly hard to satisfy the second rule because we already have too many things to do. His solution involves taking 'drastic action' to cut back on the number of projects you're working on, culling inefficient habits from your daily schedule and stopping procrastination. That's prioritisation 101. His next piece of advice is somewhat more difficult to take: risk annoying or upsetting other people in exchange for large gains in time freedom. Newport has many fans, but he's not what you'd call a people pleaser.

He advises us to take control of the demands on our time and stop being bullied by a never-ending stream of work that forces us into exhausting and inefficient schedules: 'Fix the schedule you want. Then make everything else fit around your needs.' Let's take a look at what that means in practice.

The heart of Newport's schedule is his notebook. He divides each day into 30-minute blocks and allocates time for lunch, relaxation and finishing at his pre-agreed time. Academic writer Virginia Valian devised a similar approach, along with an 'ally' for extra accountability, based on the principle of making 'friends with reality'.[22] She had a weekly scheduling session with a friend that allowed them to do their writing and to 'do our job, to ful-fil household obligations, to spend time with those we loved and liked, and to have purely frivolous time as well'. Both Newport and Valian need to write for their careers and were able to schedule it alongside other tasks that took place during the working day. By compartmentalising writing alongside their other commitments, they and other time boxers find a degree of work-life balance and avoid tussles with willpower and procrastination by following a ready-made schedule. It's effective and much beloved in time man-agement circles – those who use it, swear by its success.* However, scheduling can become a rather complicated system, and many of us can't write during the day because we have jobs and other com-mitments to attend to. A lighter version identifies slots where you can write and box them into your calendar (there's more on this at the end of the chapter).

We discovered that calendar disruptions are particularly chal-lenging for time boxers.[23] The sort of people who favour order and control find it hard when things don't go to plan, so if you take this

---

* Some advocates of time boxing take scheduling so seriously they don't like to squander a minute of their time. So called 'zero white space planners' schedule every single task in their day including hobbies, exercise and time for conversations with friends and family.

approach, acknowledge that life will get in the way at times, things will go wrong, you will be interrupted and new responsibilities will emerge. As Newport says, 'Your goal is not to stick to a given schedule at all costs; it's instead to maintain, at all times, a thoughtful say in what you are doing with your time going forward – even if those decisions are reworked again and again as the day unfolds.' While his approach is called fixed-schedule productivity, his mindset is anything but fixed. The goal is to be open to change, while keeping in mind your priorities so they don't slip. That's where noticing comes in.

NOTICING YOUR WRITING TIME

Whether you are reworking your writing schedule on a daily, weekly or monthly basis – or if you aren't using a schedule at all – notice what is happening. There is no one way to find the time to write – there are many ways, individual to each writer and their uniquely busy life. It can feel dispiriting when you realise how little time you have available to write, but rather than seek the perfect writing time, keep mindful of your circumstances and be responsive to change. It may take a while to figure out a writing routine. Newport landed on his system when still a rookie writer, while Trollope explained his with the benefit of hindsight at the very end of his writing career.

Don't remain wedded to one approach – your writing time will change as your life changes. We found that scholarly writers started out writing daily, but as they completed PhDs and their teaching responsibilities ramped up alongside family and caring roles, they switched over to time boxing; then binge writing on sabbatical kicked in at the very end of their careers when they had the privilege to take time away from administrative duties. Novelists, on the other hand, started out by scheduling writing around their commitments like a hobby or side hustle, and if they found enough success to reduce the day job they switched over to daily writing.

Likewise, how you write might change over the course of a single project. Different aspects of writing require different levels of attention and flow: like Strayed, you might retreat to go deep into a first draft, or like Selfe you could top up on writing admin while watching TV. What each of the writers featured in this chapter did was take an intentional approach to schedule, plan and prepare for their writing time, whether that was daily or a couple of times per month. That's exactly what you'll do next. The sandbox exercises that follow put into practice the theory from Part One, guiding you to notice, reflect and experiment as you figure out how to make time for writing.

The Writer's Sandbox – Time

1. SELF-ASSESSMENT: PICK AN APPROACH

Think about your current life, your work and family commitments and your other priorities over the past few months. Consider which of the descriptions best describes how you typically fit writing into your life:

> **Daily writer:** 'I need a daily writing habit and like the security of a routine.'

> **Time boxer:** 'I schedule blocks of time to write across a week or a month.'

> **Spontaneous writer:** 'I can't predict when I write; I don't need a routine of any kind.'

> **Binge writer:** 'I need long, uninterrupted periods of time to write. I like to cut myself off from the world.'

2. SEEK A SIMILAR EXAMPLE

If you haven't been writing lately, look for equivalent examples from other areas of your life where you've achieved a big goal, completed a project or implemented a new behaviour.

Examples could be starting a hobby or a new exercise regime, learning a language or musical instrument. In your work, you might have started a new job, be involved in long-term projects or had a promotion. At home, have you learned to cook, moved house, organised a wedding or large event, or had children? Perhaps you used one of these above approaches to make time.

3. RECONSIDER HOW YOU SPEND YOUR TIME

Listening to your gut is a good starting point – it can align writing with our personal values and previous experiences – but we need to get specific to create a more accurate picture. Look back on the past week or two, or longer if you're more of a binge writer, to consider what's taking your time and attention. If you use a diary or calendar, use that to review what you did. Next, imagine you could re-live that time, bearing in mind your current commitments.

- How would you re-organise your schedule? What different choices would you make?
- Were there any writing opportunities you missed? When were they?

Hindsight is indeed a wonderful thing – use it to reimagine your writing schedule. The imaginative process will create positive connections in the brain so it *feels* possible to find time.

4. LOG HOW YOU ACTUALLY SPEND YOUR TIME

Turn the previous thought experiments into a data-gathering exercise. Log how you spend your time over the coming week or so. Track your day-to-day activity as you do it to build up an accurate picture. Then go over your logs to re-evaluate what time you could have made for writing.

Time experts suggest looking at fifteen-minute intervals, though an hourly basis from when you wake to when you go to bed should give you a good enough picture.[24]

5. PLAN AHEAD – CREATE A CALENDAR FOR DAILY OR WEEKLY WRITING

If you've done one or more of the exercises above, you'll have an idea of your preference and evidence of how you might make time to write. If you plan to write daily or time box your writing across a week, the next exercise can help you schedule it in. Grab your calendar, download a blank schedule, or draw up a grid with dates across the top and your normal waking hours down the side.

- Block out all the hours that are already committed to work, care, socialising and exercise.

- What's left? Are there any opportunities? If yes, book in some time for your writing like any other appointment and commit to it – whether it's a slot every day or just once a month.
- Not found any time? Reschedule other tasks to free up time. What can you stop doing or delegate? Can you get up earlier, go to work later? This is tough, but if you want to write it needs to become a priority alongside the other important things in your life.

 Our simple time log and scheduler will help you figure out how much time you have for writing. To download them, go to: **prolifiko.com/ writtenresources**

---

6. TIME BOXING TIPS

For some writers, just having an appointment in their calendar is enough to commit. Others need more persuading, which is where pre-commitment helps. Book a writers group – in real life or online (we like Shut Up & Write!, Focusmate and Writers' Hour).[25] As writing becomes more of a priority, you will respect your writing schedule and not want to let others down by not showing up as arranged.

7. FIND YOUR DAILY WRITING ROUTINE

Daily writers overcome mental tussles with willpower by developing a habit. We take a deep dive into habits later on, but here are a few tips to get started.

- Use the logging exercise to find opportunities in your day to write.
- Find a trigger to set up the habit. This could be something you do every day such as drink coffee in the morning (and write immediately afterwards) or it could be a place or a time that sets the context to write.
- Establish the routine. Get to writing as quickly as you can. It doesn't matter if you aim to write for half an hour or target a word count; know what you are doing when you show up.

↪ Reward yourself to embed the habit– this makes it more likely you'll show up next time.

8. MASTER DELIBERATE SPONTANEITY

The key to successful spontaneity is about being prepared – that's not a contradiction! Have a list of short tasks to work on and have your notebook, laptop or a phone app with you. When an opportunity arrives, don't hesitate or procrastinate. After a few weeks, review when you wrote. You might spot patterns and be able to create a more predictable habit. Spontaneous writers dip into their work-in-progress frequently, and this method allows them to get going quickly and let go as needed.

9. BINGE WRITING FOR SUCCESS

Binge writing is about being intentional and deliberate – not about rushing for deadlines with panic-inducing, marathon-length write-ins. The sessions will be long, so identify when you can have a day or more to go deep. Work out where you can write without distraction – a library, a hotel, a friend's house or a more formal writing retreat centre. Avoid blank page blocks by knowing what you're doing – familiarise yourself in advance with your next writing task, take some writing prompts or exercises to warm up.

10. MAKING THE BEST USE OF YOUR TIME (ESPECIALLY IF YOU HAVE TOO MUCH TIME)

Once you have identified when to write, you need to make good use of that time. Whether you have ten minutes or ten hours, you can use the same technique to manage your attention. Your secret weapon is a timer.

Whether you use the Pomodoro® Technique by working in 25-minute sessions with breaks of up to five minutes, the important thing is to work without interruption.[26] If you catch yourself getting distracted, ask yourself: 'Do I need to do that *now*?' Usually you don't, so make a note of whatever popped into your head, return to your writing and keep going till the alarm sounds. Then you can consider the distracting idea or task you parked.

11. BE FLEXIBLE, BE PREPARED AND KEEP EXPERIMENTING

You might prefer one approach to making time to write, but the reality of your day-to-day life may mean you need to use a combination to move your writing forward. Be flexible, keep experimenting with different approaches, don't compare yourself to others, and most importantly don't compare yourself to an idealised future-you or a rose-tinted version of you from the past.

Use downtime between your writing sessions to research, gather ideas and make plans – there might not be time for writing, but you can keep your project in mind and make progress with related activities. Be prepared for your writing session. Have the right tools to hand (particularly if you are a spontaneous writer) and know what you are writing next so you can hit the ground running.

It's important that you reward the practice of making time and showing up to write. It will create positive associations with your writing and reduce the mental barriers to getting started. Don't feel bad when you really don't have the time to write. Life will unexpectedly get in the way – feeling guilty won't help you make progress. Instead, try a different approach to see what works. Turn that frustration into determination.

SMART

CHAPTER 4

4

GOALS

*Put your writing ambitions into words
and set the direction of travel*

'I shall be a bestselling writer.' These are the opening words of Octavia E. Butler's note to self. Written in the front cover of her spiral notebook in distinctive handwriting, this personal manifesto for success portrayed Butler's future in detail, a world where her books are read by millions of people. Have you ever committed your writing dreams to paper, outlined the prizes you'll win, the accolades, reviews and citations that will reward your efforts? If so, you're not alone. Writers are world builders by nature and their notebooks provide a glimpse into their most private wishes and unspoken ambitions. Butler's manifesto continued:

> This is my life. I write bestselling novels. My novels go onto the bestseller lists on or shortly after publication. My novels each travel up to the top of the bestseller lists and they reach the top and they stay on top for months. Each of my novels does this.

Butler's dreams first took shape aged ten, when she asked her mother to buy her a typewriter. Once in possession of a Remington, she 'pecked stories two fingered'[1] and worked on her craft as well as her typing skills. Her high-school science teacher helped her submit a story to a science-fiction magazine and throughout her life she relied on more established mentors such as science-fiction author Harlan Ellison, who was one of the first to buy her stories for an anthology he was editing.

Her early career was measured in small successes and setbacks. 'I thought I was on my way as a writer,' Butler said. 'In fact, I had five more years of rejection slips and horrible little jobs ahead of me before I sold another word.'[2] Butler worked in undemanding temporary jobs alongside writing throughout the 1970s and 1980s. By the time she wrote her note to self in 1988 she had completed her five-book *Patternist* series and was beginning to win awards for her short stories, but success was still just out of reach. When few believed in her talent, Butler backed herself.

Butler's note to self is an example of a visualisation, specifically an affirmation which is written in the present tense, as if the goal has already been achieved. As Butler affirms: 'I write bestselling novels.' This is a statement of something she wants to achieve, but framed as if it's happening already. The theory is that affirmations challenge and overcome self-limiting beliefs; by repeating them frequently, you begin to believe them, and can start to make positive changes in your life.

THE PROMISE OF POSITIVE AFFIRMATIONS

Take a simple affirmation like: 'I am a writer.' Saying you are a writer affects your self-image, and researchers have found that your self-image can influence your behaviour. Known as an 'identity pact', this association helps people stick to their decisions.[3] Let's say you decided to give up meat. Taking on a 'vegetarian' identity has been found to help you make decisions that support your meat-free choices. Vegetarians don't spend time worrying about whether to eat meat – their identity makes it easier for them to stick to their diet. So, the theory goes, calling yourself a writer can help you to write.

We find this with writers all the time. They have to write for work or study, but they don't; they have a goal, something they need to achieve, they know what to do, but they just don't do it. They come to us telling us they can't write – that's our job, helping people solve their writing problems. While 'not having time to write' often tops the list of writing problems, the next one is getting down to the writing. They tell us what they should do: 'I've got to finish my thesis ... It's important for my business to write a book ... I need to turn my stories/poems/papers/blogs into a collection.' But even with a clear goal they can't start. This chapter and the one that follows share some approaches to get you off the starting blocks. We'll begin by dreaming.

If you imagine a positive outcome, such as what it's like to achieve a long-held goal, it feels good because it triggers lots of happy-making brain chemicals. Likewise, imagining a negative outcome makes you feel bad. While the thought might be imaginary, what is going on in the brain is real, observable neurochemical reactions. And it's more than a fleeting wash of chemicals through the brain. Thinking about doing something causes new neural pathways to emerge. It's neuroplasticity in action, with the visualisation creating and changing neural networks. It could be as small as individual neurons connecting or large-scale systematic change and reorganisation. Brain plasticity is central to our development and helps us to grow, learn and recover from injuries.[4]

But therein lies the problem with positive thinking. In his 1952 book, *The Power of Positive Thinking*, Norman Vincent Peale urges us to 'Believe in yourself! Have faith in your abilities! Without a humble but reasonable confidence in your own powers you cannot be successful or happy.'[5] He describes a process of affirmations, reciting positive words and phrases as you go to sleep and first thing when you wake up. Doing so will transform every area of your life, he claims. While Peale refers to his approach as 'scientific yet simple', the book is short on science. It is, however, full of case studies that support the promise of his principles.

Like Peale, Rhonda Byrne's *The Secret* shares 'real life stories of regular people' who achieved the impossible purely by thinking and manifesting future success.[6] They are not alone in pushing positive thinking; in the summer of 2020, TikTok influencers turned manifesting into a trend.[7] A few months into the COVID-19 pandemic, with life under lockdown, the term 'manifesting' had been searched more than ever on Google.[8] Manifesting coaches schooled in the law of attraction – the belief that positive thoughts are magnets that attract wealth, health and happiness – promised outcomes based on thoughts alone.

While tales of personal transformation abound, anecdotes are not data. It is all too easy to analyse something after it has happened and create a story to explain it. This can lead to all sorts of false conclusions and lead aspiring writers to blame themselves when they fail to achieve their dreams, which is why many consider manifesting to be a dangerous pseudoscience.

UNTANGLING THE PSEUDO FROM THE SCIENCE

Researchers agree that visualising can create observable changes within the brain: that flush of feel-good when you imagine a future outcome over time creates new neural pathways. But can this help us perform better?

In sports, visualising helps players to rehearse for an event or competition. When elite athletes were training for the 2020 Olympics during the COVID-19 lockdown, they didn't have access to training facilities, so increasingly relied on 'at home' visualisations as a form of practice. British Olympic dive champion and knitting enthusiast Tom Daley explained: 'I visualise myself competing my dives when I'm not able to compete,'[9] calling this type of mental rehearsal 'awesome' as the power of the mind kept him competition-ready even when he was unable to train.[10] He went on to win a bronze and a gold medal at the event. Studies looking at golfers identified a combination of training approaches, where golfers take practice shots on a real-life golf course, rehearse the shots in their head and also observe other players. One study found that watching other golfers practise can trigger the creation of neural pathways.[11] And the benefits don't just accrue to the players – golf caddies have an ability beyond their training and practice hours from their close proximity to expertise. That got us thinking about some of the classic writing advice about the importance of reading: does reading help you write better?* The explanation lies with 'mirror neurons' firing when we observe or simulate practice. The mirror neurons behave as if an observed experience were actually real.

Back to the evidence. If the brain cannot differentiate between a real experience and an observed or even an imagined one, can we benefit from them in the same way? Psychologists have studied a range of domains, most often sport but also music[12] and rehabilitation, to investigate whether mental practice is able to support and enhance performance. While a consensus exists about the benefits, these have been hard to measure. The term 'mental practice' is vague, meaning that studies looking at it include a variety of cognitive rehearsal approaches, making it hard to compare like with like.[13] In one meta-analysis, the results indicated that 'mental practice has a positive and significant effect on performance'.

---

* What about watching writers write? There hasn't been a study into writers, though we're having fun imagining a writers' version of Twitch, the video game live streaming site where gamers watch others play.

Of course, there are caveats such as type of task, how long it is practised for, and the time between practice and performance, but the study shows that mental practice works.[14] The important thing is to do it with purpose: idle daydreaming doesn't cut it. To be effective, the mental rehearsal needs to be as deliberate as a physical practice would be, for example including planning, self-evaluation, identification of problems and subsequent correction of mistakes. There is more on deliberate practice and self-coaching later on. For now, let's consider how visualising can, under some conditions, help you write better.

FROM MINDSET TO ACTION

When Octavia E. Butler wrote her affirmation of being a best-selling author, she was a struggling writer with crappy day jobs. Her childhood dream to tell stories had been battered by years of rejection and prejudice. Butler went on to become the first science-fiction writer to win a MacArthur Genius Grant, and received the PEN American Center lifetime achievement award in writing as well as multiple awards including Hugo and Nebula prizes. Her books are read by millions and include perennial sellers like *Kindred*. The mother of Afro-Futurism, she became one of the most influential writers of her time and increased access to privileged literary spaces.[15] The MacArthur prize of $295,000 helped her realise her dreams of getting healthcare for her and her mother, buying a 'beautiful' home in an 'excellent' neighbourhood, and being able to hire a car whenever she wanted to. All of these things are imagined in her note to self, along with her desire to support others: 'I will send poor black youngsters to Clarion or other writers' workshops. I will help poor black youngsters broaden their horizons. I will help poor black youngsters go to college.'

Butler's note is a compelling story – a struggling author writes down her dreams and within ten years she has achieved them. But there is more to her affirmations than words; it's self-talk that primes her for action. She writes: 'I will find the way to do this. See to it! So be it! See to it!' While mindset is important, you need action to translate those dreams into reality. Butler had a clear vision for her future and meticulously planned her writing career by developing her craft and her network (areas we'll explore later in this book). In short, she had a goal, she put in place a plan, and she persevered to achieve it.

● ● ●

Humans are goal-setting creatures – we can't help but hope something will happen in the future. We believe things can change for the better; whether that's wishing for sunshine tomorrow, dreaming of a birthday present, or fighting for an end to injustice. That's where goal-setting comes in – turning those hopes into plans. Understanding how goal-setting works can help translate your writing dreams into reality.

In the 1960s, psychologist Edwin Locke explained the link between goals, motivation and performance on which so much modern productivity advice is based. Most goal-setting research has focussed on employee performance (hello capitalism) but the findings are applicable to other settings. Having goals affects performance in four ways, Locke explains, 'by directing attention, mobilizing effort, increasing persistence, and motivating strategy development'.[16]

It's pretty obvious, but worth stating, that having goals helps us to prioritise. By directing us away from unrelated activities, goals allow us to focus on the tasks that contribute to achieving our dreams. For Butler, her priority was writing rather than a career which would have distracted her and used up valuable time and mental energy. Goals are energising – as we saw earlier, just imagining a future state fires up the brain. A few years ago when Bec's writing group planned to publish a collection of short stories, they shared the excitement of making that happen. Motivation helps with persistence as we work harder to achieve what we set out to do. It also encourages us to learn new skills in pursuit of our dreams – as you know, writing requires attention to craft. Goals can push us beyond our current capability. But there's a formula for successful goal-setting.

HOW TO SET SUCCESSFUL GOALS

Locke uncovered the sweet spot of setting goals that are difficult and specific. In one meta-analysis he found that 'in 90 per cent of the studies, specific and challenging goals led to higher performance than easy goals, "do your best" goals, or "no goals"'. Locke partnered with Dr Gary Latham and together they published the now seminal text *A Theory of Goal-Setting and Task Performance*, which outlined five characteristics for successful goal-setting.[17] These are:

1. Clarity – goals need to be specific on what to do and by when.
2. Challenge – goals must balance being difficult yet also attainable.
3. Commitment – goals must be set by the individual and accepted.
4. Feedback – there has to be some way of measuring progress.
5. Task complexity – complex or long-term goals should be broken down into smaller, manageable steps.

The point of visualising success is to imagine a future beyond your current trajectory. Otherwise, why bother? Your dream will by definition feel impossible and beyond reach, which can leave you feeling overwhelmed, stuck and unable to make a start. The key to turning mindset into action is something that psychologists call 'optimum motivational goals' – ones that spur you on, but don't overwhelm you. A neat combination of challenge and specificity that Locke and Latham tell us we need.

● ● ●

Bernardine Evaristo is an experimental prose poet who writes literary fiction. When she started writing in the 1980s, her work was not at all mainstream or of interest to commercial publishers. While she wrote 'into the void'[18] she harboured big ambitions. She developed a positive mental attitude as a coping tactic against the neglect of Black British writing, especially the sort of radical fiction she favoured. Immersing herself in self-help and personal development, Evaristo began a habit of affirmations that turned her ambition into a vision where she achieved impossible goals: 'I understood that goals within easy reach aren't a vision at all, but merely a next stage, a small step.'

When her first prose book *Lara* was published in 1997, she wrote an affirmation about winning the Booker Prize. 'Even when the odds were stacked against me, I have believed that somehow, some day, I'd break through.' She continued to write experimental literary fiction for over twenty years until her 2019 novel *Girl, Woman, Other* won the Booker Prize and stayed in the top-ten bestseller charts for 44 weeks. Evaristo warns that 'manifestations don't work if you don't do the work'. She's right. The danger of positive thinking is that it can make you feel like you've already done the work (there's more on this in Chapter 6). Now, even though she has achieved everything that she dreamed of and more, Evaristo still writes an affirmation for each new book she works on, as doing so pumps her up 'with confidence and commitment'. Doing this fills her with energy and positivity, motivating her for the task ahead.

Evaristo meets each of Locke and Latham's five characteristics for successful goal-setting. She also demonstrates how optimum motivational goals work by making you feel pumped up and positive about the project ahead. You can apply this in your own goal-setting by having a stretch goal – a big dream that sparks ambition – and a specific goal to help you form a plan.

We've explored what it means to dream big – now it's time to get specific.

SMARTEN YOUR GOALS

You might have encountered SMART goal-setting in the workplace. This mnemonic acronym* is drummed into managers to help them set quarterly targets. If you aren't traumatised by HR training, it provides a simple yet effective structure that ticks all the boxes for successful goal-setting. Bonus: it even gets the backing of our goal-setting gurus Locke and Latham. Here's how to smarten up your dreams.

Specific

Vague goals lead to vague outcomes. Getting specific helps define what you need to do to accomplish your desired endpoint. Start by being clear about what you want to achieve. Don't say: 'I must write more.' Instead define what you mean by 'writing'. Is it word-on-page

---

* Although the letters have come to stand for different things over time, which rather defeats the purpose of it as a memory prompt.

drafting, or time with your project to read, research and plan? And what does 'more' mean – is that more words, more often, or for longer? Being specific can refer to dates, times, or places where you commit to writing, so think about what this might look like in your life – for example, what opportunities there are for writing, and when and where can you write at home/work/somewhere else?

Measurable

You can't manage what you can't measure. A goal such as 'I'll write more over the next few weeks' makes it impossible to know if it's been achieved. Instead, 'I'll write 500 words each writing session' or 'I'll write three times a week' helps you to monitor your progress and know whether you have achieved your goal. How your goal should be measured is completely up to you, but keeping track is a great way to see what's possible and chart your progress. You can then use the data to edit and reframe your goal along the way.

Achievable

For your goal to be successful it must be attainable. Over-ambitious goals can lead to overwhelm and panic, while under-ambitious ones can lead to boredom, procrastination and delay. Let's say you are aiming for a particular word count per session – can you write 2,000 words or 250? Be realistic and remember that it takes practice to work out what's achievable (which is why measurement helps root it in reality).

Relevant

Your goals should align with what you set out to achieve. This might sound rather obvious, but spending all your time writing haikus if your actual goal is to write a thesis isn't the best idea. Focus on the overall objective and what's needed to achieve it to avoid distraction. Think of your dream or ambition like a North Star guiding you towards a destination. Check that what you are doing contributes towards it. If you are writing 'more', is it a specific project goal such a writing a book, or is it a practice goal where you write three times a week on a range of different projects?

Timed

Deadlines improve the effectiveness of goals. Without a time frame and some pressure, there will be no urgency to act. They might not be pleasant, but they will increase your focus and direct your limited energy. Again, it takes practice to figure out how long things take, so monitor your progress and adjust as you go. What is a suitable timeline for you? If you have a long-term ambition, set a final date (even if it's a rough estimate) and then add in milestones along the way to break the goal down.

According to Locke and Latham, goals are 'immediate regulators of behavior', creating a sense of self and a vision of what's possible that can prompt motivation for action.[19] Visualising is no substitute for the hard work of writing, but it's a starting point. In her notebook Butler set herself a challenging goal, one which was exciting and motivating – a stretch goal. Pairing a stretch goal (dream) with a specific (SMART) plan puts the impossible within reach. Aim for the tingle factor, that buzz of motivation you get from imagining the future where you achieve your goals. Plus, only having a few big dreams helps you prioritise what you're working on and stops distraction from smaller, easier and less important tasks.

ALL GOOD THINGS MUST BEGIN

As writers we're often told: 'Follow your dreams and never stop dreaming until those dreams come true.' But that advice is 'crap' according to showrunner, screenwriter and author Shonda Rhimes.[20] She says that a lot of people dream and 'while they are busy dreaming, the really happy people, the really successful people, the really interesting, powerful, engaged people? Are busy doing.' That's why Butler's notebooks provide a valuable insight into the creative process.* Reading them alongside her biography, we can track the progress of her dreams with her output. Butler does not provide a commentary on why she wrote her note or what function it played in her life; however, in reading it we can see a precise picture of the future she imagined for her writing and publishing success. She wrote in detail of what her writing would achieve for her, her family and also how she would pay it forward to her community.

There is no doubt that Butler went on to achieve exactly what she visualised all those years ago. We can find encouragement in her journal entries and understand that naming her goals was an essential step in her journey towards success. Together with Bernardine Evaristo, she provides the inspiration and practical approach to get the writing done. We'll look at this in more detail in the next chapter. Before you start taking steps, you need to put your beliefs and ambitions into words, name your goal and set the direction of travel. The sandbox exercises that follow are designed to get your neurons firing and gear you up for writing by getting pumped about the future; they will help you dream big and stretch your ambition, as well as get specific by going SMART. As Butler wrote in her notebook: 'All good things must begin.'

---

* The realisation of Butler's dreams was the culmination of a lifetime's work and is catalogued in journals and papers going back to her school days. This treasure trove sits alongside first drafts of her work, photos and memorabilia in the Huntington Library in San Marino, California, where scholars can explore her archive and gain unique insight into a writer's inner process.

The Writer's Sandbox – Goals

1. SIMPLE AFFIRMATIONS

Affirmations are positive statements, written in the present tense, that challenge self-limiting beliefs. By repeating them frequently, you begin to believe them, which can help you to make positive changes in your life. We can't manifest success, but we can set an intention for ourselves as writers or for each project. Writing an affirmation is a quick first step in identifying as a writer and working towards your writing goals.

2. VISUALISE YOUR GOALS

Visualising your writing goals gives you something to aim towards – you need to know your destination to chart a route there.

Start by noting down your writing goal. Put into words what you want to achieve. At this stage, don't worry about making it specific – that will come. Instead look for the feeling of anticipation when you have an exciting challenge ahead of you.

You can use visual tools to craft your visualisation. Cara Holland, a visual-thinking recorder, author and illustrator of this book says that 'visioning, the act of imagining and drawing the future, can help bring clarity to your ambition'.[21] One of the most popular exercises in Julia Cameron's *The Artist's Way* is making a collage.[22] Grab a pencil and piece of paper and sketch out your writing dreams and goals. It will embed the message deeper and help you retain it more clearly and for longer.

3. VISUALISE SUCCESS

If you imagine a positive outcome, such as what it's like to achieve a long-held goal, it feels good because it triggers lots of positive brain chemicals. Neuroscience shows that when you visualise something, you stimulate the same parts of the brain as when you actually do it, causing new neural pathways to emerge. This process of neuroplasticity is central to our development.

Write a list of all the good things that will happen when you achieve your goal. What will you think? What will you do? What will you say? How will you feel? What will the outcome be? One neuroscientist we worked with suggested writing a list of 50 things.[23] It sounds tough, but it will get your brain in gear and flushed with feel-good emotions.

4. OPTIMUM MOTIVATIONAL GOAL – STRETCH AND SPECIFIC
Write your goal as a simple sentence. You are aiming for a stretch, so push beyond what you are capable of right now.

Next, get specific in order to create a plan. Using SMART, make your goal specific, measurable, achievable, relevant and timed.

5. CHECK YOUR GOAL FOR THE TINGLE FACTOR
Once you've set a writing goal, check in with yourself to see how it makes you feel. Ask, is your goal:

a) Overwhelming and daunting?
b) Like it will be a walk in the park?
c) Exciting, challenging but also achievable?

If you chose a) it's likely that you'll never start because over-ambitious goals can lead to procrastination – make your goal smaller. If you chose b) it's likely you'll switch off before you've finished – push yourself a little more. If you chose c) you're in the sweet spot. You've found the tingle factor: a goal that's a little bit challenging, but not so much that it feels daunting.

6. REVISIT YOUR GOALS
A final important part of all the exercises is being reminded of your dreams and goals.

Octavia E. Butler wrote hers in the front cover of her spiral notebook. Bernardine Evaristo writes an affirmation for every new project and stores her past dreams in a trunk. You can simply write yours on a Post-it note and stick it on your computer or type it into your screen-saver. If you want reminding, set a calendar notification. For example, Bec checks her goals on the date of her birthday each month. You can even write a letter to future you[23] and get reminded in a few years' time.

Remember that your goal is neither fixed nor set in stone. Change it to suit your project and where you are in your life. Some goals will work for you and others won't. How you write will change over time depending on the other things going on in your life. Be flexible with how you approach your goal and try not to compare your approach to anyone else's – or how you might have written before.

 Our writing goals planner helps you name your dream, make it SMART and identify a first step. To download it, go to: **prolifiko. com/writtenresources**

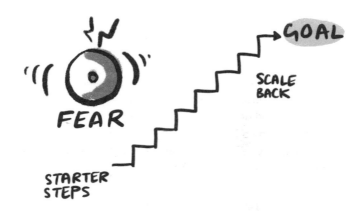

GOAL

SCALE
BACK

FEAR

STARTER
STEPS

CHAPTER 5

5

STARTING

Momentum leads to motivation:
start small and progress will follow

It's the first day of November. The morning is chilled with frost. The buckets of sugary treats gifted the night before have lost their appeal. Once magnificently scary Halloween costumes are now fit for the dry cleaners – or the recycling bin. For some, the events calendar has shifted to Bonfire Night or Diwali. For others, the night drawing in, air tinged with sulphurous fireworks, signals the arrival of an audacious month-long event. Writers the world over fire up their computers, roll up their sleeves and face the task of writing 1,667 words a day, every day for 30 days. It's National Novel Writing Month (NaNoWriMo) and in 2021 Bec joined the writers on the starting line, aiming to complete a 50,000 word novel by the time November was out. The first day she was raring to go, pumped full of motivation and armed with a rock-solid plan to hit the goal. She motored for the first week, aided by a pre-arranged writing retreat where she binge wrote a frankly obscene number of words in four days. But once home, real life hit her with full force. *A few days off won't hurt*, she thought, but a couple of days turned to a week, and before she knew it, she was thousands of words behind schedule with no way to catch up.

She abandoned her goal.

You might be familiar with this experience: a once super-tasty goal quickly turns sour. It hits many of us in January when our 'New Year, New You' resolutions come to nought. In the last chapter, we advocated for dreaming big to build motivation for writing. Yet, there is more to motivation than the tingle factor you feel when visualising the future. In fact, the tingle factor can trick us into thinking we've already achieved our goal and make us less motivated to act. While it is true that having a big ambitious goal can excite us, the irony is that it's more likely to lead to inaction rather than the required action. There's more on the science of this in the next chapter, so hold that thought. For now it's enough to understand that a large goal stimulates our body's fight or flight mechanism, and the more important that goal is, and the more riding on the outcome, the greater the feeling of fear becomes until it overwhelms us. The once-exciting goal feels unachievable, leading to procrastination, delay and often failure.[1]

Hundreds of thousands of people sign up to NaNoWriMo. With 20 per cent smashing their goal, it goes to show that going big does work for some. However, if you fall with the 80 per cent who fail to reach the target, this chapter explores a different approach to making progress; a solution that works whether you're starting a project or finishing one, whether you're a rookie writer or a veteran. It's the advice we give to every writer at all stages of the writing process – and it works. But before we tell you how to harness this approach, we'll meet a remarkable woman who took on the huge goal of writing about racism.

Layla F. Saad was an avid user of Instagram. She'd built a community of 19,000 followers to her account where she shared posts on female spirituality and leadership. In August 2017, news of a white nationalist rally in Charlottesville USA left her reeling, especially when she noticed that no one in her community was talking about it. She channelled her shock into writing a blog post.[2]

One night, almost a year later, she lay awake wondering what her community had learned. 'That was the spark,' she said. She started writing notes on her phone.[3] At first it was a single question that she was going to 'throw out' on Instagram, but she soon realised it was going to be more than a single post. Saad announced that she was going to do a 28-day Instagram challenge and asked her followers to join her. She woke the next day full of dread, doubting whether it was a good idea.

START SMALL

Millennia ago, Chinese philosopher Lao Tzu wrote: 'Confront the difficult while it is still easy; accomplish the great task by a series of small acts.'[4] Tackling white supremacism is certainly difficult. Saad approached it by asking a series of seemingly small questions that started a big conversation with people at an individual level. When she opened the photo-sharing app the next day, there was a stream of comments under her post. People were up for it. 'OK,' she said, 'let's go.'[5]

Whether your goal requires plucking up the courage to post on social media, put a blog into the world or write a book, it all begins with that first step. Just like Saad doubting her decision to post on Instagram, we've been psychologically programmed to avoid doing scary things. The solution to overcoming your fight or flight response is to focus on small actions that don't engage these primitive survival responses. Having a smaller focus bypasses the fear centres of the brain. Psychologist Dr Robert Maurer explains:

> Small easily achievable goals let you tiptoe past your amygdala, keeping it asleep and unable to set off alarm bells.

As your small steps continue and the cortex starts working, the brain begins to create software for your desired change, actually laying down new nerve pathways and building new habits.[6]

Not only can thinking small avoid triggering the fear centres of the brain, it creates new neural networks to support writing habits longer term. This is far more effective than relying on motivation to get us started or willpower to keep us going. Although dreaming big is vital to visualise your success, it's the smaller goals along the way that will help you get there.

In psychological terms, motivation is wanting something such as a change in behaviour – like writing more or procrastinating less. It's often described as a drive or a need, something 'inside' us that desires change. It's that feeling we get when we visualise success – excited, driven, pumped full of action-oriented and goal-directed energy. However, motivation is a very poor predicator of building successful habits. We'd go so far as to say it's a booby trap, and one many of us are likely to fall into, perhaps a few days after setting a New Year's resolution, signing up to ambitious writing challenges or sending off an application for a place on a doctorate programme.

MOTIVATION – OUR FICKLE FRIEND

While motivation is an important driver of change, it is unreliable. Stanford-based social science researcher B.J. Fogg refers to motivation as being like a party-animal friend, someone who is great on a night out but not one you would rely on for anything important. As well as being fickle, our motivations are often in conflict; anyone who has had to grapple with multi-year goals, like writing a book while maintaining some kind of work-life balance, will know exactly what we mean.

Fogg created a simple yet powerful model to explain the relationship between motivation and our ability to act. The Fogg Behavior Model[7] helps us to understand what's going on in those first days of a New Year's writing resolution or an attempt to hit a daily NaNoWriMo target – or indeed any ambitious goal. Behaviour happens when three things come together at the same time: motivation, ability and prompt. It's often written out as B=MAP, where:

- B is behaviour – the thing you want to do, namely writing.
- M is motivation – our fickle friend, this mysterious internal driver to act.
- A is ability – our capacity to do the action, which might require skill and aptitude.
- P is prompt – the trigger that prompts us to do the behaviour.

The Fogg Behavior Model is shown as a graph, with motivation for a behaviour on the vertical axis running from low to high, and ability

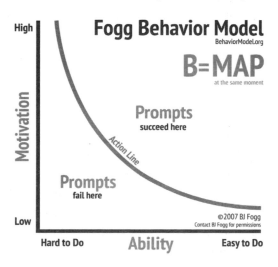

to do the behaviour on the horizontal axis ranging from hard to easy to do. The curved line is called the 'action line', and it explains the relationship between motivation and ability. When the action you need to take is very hard, like writing a book, screenplay or thesis, you need a lot of motivation. However, when the action is easy to do, like writing a sentence, you can get by with low levels of motivation. This line determines how likely something is to become a behaviour, with success marked on one side and failure on the other side.

Take the example of getting up an hour earlier to write. This is hard for most people and would require iron-cast motivation to do once, let alone repeat enough to become a regular routine. However, finding five minutes to write during the day is easier to do and needs a far lower level of motivation. Likewise, hitting 1,667 words a day for NaNoWriMo is achievable in perfect circumstances, but one or two slips requires more motivation to catch up – and keep going!

According to Fogg, because motivation is so darned fickle, we can't rely on it to show up, let alone remain high. That means when we want to do something, our best approach is to make the tasks as easy as possible. Once we start doing an easy task, repetition builds skills; cumulatively the behaviour becomes easier to do, so you can ramp it up to build a habit (more on this later).

The final part of the equation is having a prompt, a trigger that gets us to do the new behaviour. Often these can be found in things we do already and automatically, such as getting up, starting or finishing work, or eating meals. Each of these are great prompts for action. Take another of Bec's goals:* to read more non-fiction

---

* Bec, as you might have realised, loves goals, challenges and developing new habits and behaviours. Chris less so. We'll explore how and why we are so different in Chapter 9.

books. Like many people, her prompt to read was going to bed, but tackling a weighty research-heavy tome just kept her mind buzzing and only lead to bouts of insomnia. She experimented with using breakfast as a trigger to read non-fiction, while keeping bedtime for novels. As well as doubling her reading, there was the bonus of swapping out a breakfast bad habit of doomscrolling the day's news over coffee and porridge. Using prompts, she developed a behaviour that met a goal of reading more by removing the call to willpower and replacing it with an easy task – and a clear prompt – that removes the requirement for motivation. Reading is what happens at those times and over time it became a habit.

START WITH A FIRST STEP

Fogg's research with over 60,000 people found that anyone can develop a new behaviour, however ambitious, if they start tiny. He shares the story of his failure to create a flossing habit even though he needed and wanted to floss. Using Tiny Habits® his first step was to floss one tooth. It was the small, easy-to-do start he needed to develop his flossing behaviour.

For Layla F. Saad, her step was posting a question on Instagram. Let's see how it turned out for her. The morning after she shared her intention, people were up for the challenge. Over the next 28 days, her community followed the hashtag #MeAndWhiteSupremacy to address a different question publicly in the comments and privately by journalling. She thought people would leave, but every day more people flocked in and it continued to grow. She explains: 'After six months I turned the challenge into a workbook and expanded it and put it into the world as a free downloadable workbook and that also went viral. Within three days, more than 11,000 people had downloaded it and within six months nearly 100,000 people had downloaded it.'[8]

Within a month of self-publishing, she'd been approached by major international publishing houses asking if she wanted to turn it into a book. And that's exactly what she did. Saad published *Me and White Supremacy* in 2020. Her book debuted at number eight on the *New York Times* bestseller list and third on the *Sunday Times* bestseller list, reaching number five on the *NYT* bestseller list later that summer. The experience was life-changing for Saad, who describes the initial 28-day challenge as being 'profoundly heart-breaking and heart-expanding'.[9] What started with a social media post ended up hitting the bestseller lists on both sides of the Atlantic. Saad describes the journey as a 'quantum leap'[10] – a leap that began with one small step.

As Lao Tzu said: 'A journey of a thousand miles must start with the first step.'[11] Once you know what behaviour you want to build, such as writing regularly, you need to identify the smallest possible way to start. There are two approaches for this.[12]

1. **Starter step.** This will be something very small that gets you going, such as opening your notebook or naming a document. It's not necessarily about doing any writing – yet. It will develop into a writing habit, but by keeping the first step small you'll be able to begin.

2. **Scaling back.** This approach gets you to look at the behaviour you want, like working daily on your 70,000-word novel, and shrinking it. So rather than write 1,000 words per session, write ten. Turn up every day, repeat and the routine will build. Over time you'll increase how many words you write.

Failure to make progress on your big goal has nothing to with character failure or a lack of willpower or self-discipline. Saad's book is a brilliant example of scaling back: she took the massive problem of people engaging meaningfully in conversations about race and began by asking a series of small questions. Her Instagram posts grew to become a self-published workbook and then a bestselling book which achieved her original aim of changing the conversation. Let's look at the other approach of 'starter steps'.

PECKING AWAY

When Fogg was experimenting with floss at Stanford University, on the other side of the San Francisco Bay an employee of an exciting new startup was taking some small steps with his writing. In 2007, Robin Sloan was one of the first employees at Twitter. His job was to convince traditional media companies, like TV stations, that Twitter might be helpful for their news reporting because it tapped into emerging citizen journalism by providing real-time updates to breaking stories. While his work was fun, chaotic and very demanding, it was also frustrating because Sloan wanted to create content himself, not just report on other people's.

'If I had to put my finger on the absolutely transformative and lucky encounter,' he said, 'it might be that we formed a little writing group.' Sloan explains that he and two friends would meet every week with the agreement that they had to bring something for the others to read and discuss. Because of the tight turnaround, they wrote and shared very short passages, what he called 'fragments', that could be the beginning of a story or a piece of flash fiction.

One day Sloan was scrolling through Twitter (after all, that was his job) when he read a tweet from @idlethink who had mistaken a sign for a 24-hour book drop as a 24-hour bookshop.[13] Inspiration struck and he explored this prompt in his next writing fragment. It sparked a story idea, and after a few months of writing and getting feedback and support from his writing group, he completed a short story of 6,000 words. With that milestone completed, his motivation was high and he was eager for his next step.

Amazon had just released its first Kindle e-reader, and Sloan was in love with it: 'I encountered that device and thought, "Oh, this is seductive. This is beautiful. What can I pour into this strange new container?"' He decided to self-publish his story *Mr. Penumbra's 24-Hour Bookstore*.[14] The story sold around 1,000 copies on the Kindle Store. For a first-time writer-slash-publisher it was incredible success. He had written something, put it out into the world, and strangers were paying to read it! He was hooked and wanted to write and publish more.

In 2009, a new development in technology caught Sloan's eye. It was the crowdfunding platform Kickstarter, which people were using to raise funds to support creative projects. In late August, Sloan set up a page called 'Robin writes a book (and you get a copy)'[15] and started hustling for backers – his goal was to get 300 people to support him. Kickstarter has a fixed period for running fundraising campaigns, so the clock was ticking. He shared with friends, family and his small audience of readers and the word slowly got round. By October he had 422 backers and was featured on the Kickstarter home page – the dream for every project. By the time the campaign ended at midnight on 31 October 2009, Sloan had 570 backers who pledged $13,942. The project was successfully funded, and to make things interesting, he decided to write the novella at the same time as running the campaign. That meant within a week of completion he had proof copies of the book, and a fortnight later everyone received a copy, just as promised. While that's great, that's not the whole story. The Kickstarter campaign caught the attention of an agent who was after a novel. Sloan explains:

We sat and we schemed and we decided that there was a bigger story waiting in *Penumbra*'s shadowy shelves. So in 2010, I started working on my first full-length novel. 2010 passed and I pecked away at *Penumbra*. It wasn't until the last possible minute – literally the stroke of midnight on New Year's Eve – that I finished the first draft. It was rough to read, hard to understand – but it was the whole story, start to finish. And we went from there.[16]

His first draft of *Mr. Penumbra's 24-Hour Bookstore* made it to his agent, onwards to a publisher, to bookshops and into enough readers' hands to get it onto the *New York Times* bestseller list. It was one of the *San Francisco Chronicle*'s best 100 books of 2012, a *New York Times* Editor's Choice, as well as making the NPR Hardcover Fiction Bestseller list. All from an idea triggered by a tweet.

MORE APPROACHES TO MAKING PROGRESS

Sloan, in his words, was pecking away with 'starter steps' by writing short fragments that built his experience and skills as he found more opportunities to share his work with readers. Saad 'scaled back', taking a massive problem and making a dent in it by working with her community on a daily challenge. Neither of them had goals in the traditional sense of aiming for a specific target, such as trying to get on to the *New York Times* bestseller list – which they both did. Both are great examples of how to make progress in small steps. They figured out how to start, which is the important thing, and continued in a way that was meaningful and manageable for them.

For some professions, the approach is more intentional and writers are trained to use incremental stages. In academic writing this is called 'scaffold publishing'. Scaffolding is the process where researchers might first present their ideas at a conference, then they submit a journal article or perhaps write a short-form book for publication. They don't start by writing a weighty monograph. Instead they take smaller, incremental steps. Technology has made this easier. Many academics embrace digital forms which can be as simple as blogging, creating YouTube videos or using TikTok as the way to share ideas and build a following (check out #academics).

The UKSG, a UK-based charity that supports scholarly communications, said: 'This scaffolding of publications approach enables researchers to meet institutional expectations while also leveraging more creative avenues to share and grow potential for next steps in their research.'[17] It helps academics deal with the 'publish or perish' pressure from their university institutions while focussing on creativity which can, for many, be a highly satisfying part of the writing process.

Before we all abandon our books and head to TikTok, let's learn from other writers who take a considered approach to planning steps, such as entrepreneurs who write. They are in a position to apply their professional know-how to a creative practice like writing, breaking a goal down into smaller milestones in the same way they might forecast income or work on a product roadmap. For those who share their expertise by blogging, contributing articles for industry press or working on a book, writing is a core part of their business plan. This is an approach recommended by Alison Jones, director of Practical Inspiration Publishing. Rather than seeing writing as an output or final stage of a longer process of learning and thinking, she views it as a valuable tool to support thinking at every stage.

However, when Jones came to write her own book, she froze. Her primal fight or flight response kicked in. She explains: 'When

I wrote *This Book Means Business* I came up against massive imposter syndrome: writing a book about writing a book is a cripplingly self-conscious exercise.' Jones needed a way into writing which made the most of her personality and would help her tiptoe past her crippling fear of the page. After some reflection, she found her first step:

> I launched The Extraordinary Business Book Club podcast explicitly as a way to make myself publicly accountable for writing the book, as well as a platform for speaking to experts to get their tips and insights. This turned out to be a brilliant strategy for me personally because I'm an extrovert: I get my energy from connecting and engaging with others, not sitting alone with a keyboard.

Often a first step in writing isn't actual writing. For Jones, her podcast gave a regular pipeline of content for her book and the accountability structure to show up each week and do the work. She's not alone in finding a way into her writing which isn't just about words on the page. Take Charles Dickens, author of fifteen novels as well as numerous short stories, essays, articles and novellas. He fuelled his writing in dialogue with others – with long talks and walks with fellow authors, lengthy correspondence with fans, and writing serialisations. These are all staged approaches to writing that provide inspiration and feedback in small and enjoyable tasks.

For many of us, these activities could become procrastination – endlessly talking about writing rather than writing. Key to making this approach work is that all the parts lead up to something greater. For Jones, talking to experts helped her figure out what to write; she blogged about the podcast and then used these posts as the basis for her book. Likewise, Dickens harnessed serialisation, a form of episodic writing where instalments are written and published in magazines before the works are compiled and republished as full-length novels. His first novel, *The Pickwick Papers*, was commissioned as a monthly feature in a popular periodical of the time and was published in nineteen episodes alongside comic illustrations. He had never written a novel before, so being asked to submit a monthly column provided a way in. It was such a successful tactic for him that he founded a magazine called *Household Words* to give him a platform to share his writing. He was a pioneer who inspired many of his contemporaries to follow his example, including George Eliot, William Makepeace Thackeray and Elizabeth Gaskell who all grew huge audiences from their serialised stories.[18]

Publishing in a serial fashion meant Dickens got feedback from his audience and he rewrote plots, changed characters and improved the structure and suspense of his work based on readers' responses. While magazines have fallen out of fashion, serialisation exists in other formats and is used by writers to great success. E.L. James started writing an erotic fanfiction blog that honoured the *Twilight* series of novels by Stephenie Meyer. She wrote at night after her day job working in TV, writing frantically and posting updates to meet the demand from her fans. The story was originally called 'Master of the Universe' but James rewrote the story into the *Fifty Shades* trilogy over eighteen months. She published in 2011 with a small Australian publisher before a bidding frenzy that led to sales of 150 million copies and a worldwide phenomenon with translations into 50 languages.[19]

HOW TO SET SUBGOALS

Scaffolding and serialisation are ways of breaking down large goals into smaller stages, what researchers call 'proximal subgoals' – the opposite of distal goals, which are the far-away dreams we might have. Not only can taking a staged approach avoid triggering the fear centres of the brain so we get things done, it results in a big uptick in motivation. Psychologists researching learning in the 1970s found that setting incremental subgoals has positive psychological effects.

1. Close-by goals provide immediate incentives in performance compared with far-away ones where people tend to slacken their efforts.
2. They help people better understand what needs doing, allowing them to choose what activities to do, how much effort is required, and how long they will persist.
3. Through meeting their subgoals, people make progress and are more likely to master the skills involved.

Subgoals increase motivation and make it more likely that people will continue with the project at hand, according to researchers Albert Bandura and Dale H. Schunk: 'When people aim for, and master, desired levels of performance, they experience a sense of satisfaction. The satisfaction derived from subgoal attainments can build intrinsic interest.'[20] It's a win-win: not only will setting small steps make you more likely to do them and to keep going, it also makes you feel rather good. Momentum leads to motivation, rather than the other way round. Which leads us to our final piece of good news.

Many of the examples used in this chapter are of people who wanted to write, who were already motivated to do something, whether for their own pleasure, their career or business, or as a form of activism to changes hearts and minds. What if, for example, you don't really want to write? Then take heart, the researchers have you covered. Rather than look into the dream-fulfilment type of goal,

Bandura and Schunk sought people who had no interest in the activity. They found that even when people had a 'strong disinterest' in studying, they could manage self-directed learning over a series of sessions by having incremental goals.

Whenever you get stuck, lose heart in your current project and can't bear to continue, set aside motivation and instead go small.

● ● ●

All the writers in this chapter found a way to bypass the fear centres of the brain with a small step that led to progress on their goals. Alison Jones tapped into her extrovert energy with a podcast; Layla F. Saad worked with her community on Instagram; Charles Dickens wrote serialisations; Robin Sloan formed a writing group with two buddies to share fragments; and academics get going by scaffolding their writing projects in incremental stages. Each of these writers found a way in that worked for them. While you might want to borrow one of their steps, it is far better to find your own personal approach. We encourage writers to brainstorm options using a simple two-step process – here's how:

1. Generate several options, because the best way to have a good idea is to have lots of ideas.
2. Pick the one that is quickest, easiest or the most fun to do.

While some productivity advice focusses on swallowing a frog first thing in the morning,* we find the best way to get started is to do

---

* 'If it's your job to eat a frog, it's best to do it first thing in the morning. And if it's your job to eat two frogs, it's best to eat the biggest one first.' This advice is widely attributed to Mark Twain, though no evidence exists of him actually saying it. In something you enjoy – and the research backs this up.[21] So once you've brainstormed all the small ways you can get started and scale back your big goal, it's time to consider which is the smallest step, the speediest or most simple to do. Think of something you can do now or later today; if none of them can be done in just a few minutes, it's a signal to scale back even further. Remember, you are looking for really small steps such as opening your notebook, naming a new document or writing a sentence or two. Once you've got a few to choose from, pick the one that appeals to you the most.

That's exactly what Robin Sloan does. Rather than have a deliberate daily writing practice every day, he tries to have some fun with writing. It might be putting something into a manuscript, writing for his newsletter, a blog post, or self-publishing a novella – there are so many options. He explains: 'Writing can also be fun, matter-of-fact, rushed, bonkers, commercial, crass – and totally successful. Anything can work. Not everything does! But the gates of the city are wide open and there are a thousand ways in.'[22]

Let's find your way in.

2007 Brian Tracy published *Eat That Frog!: 21 Great Ways to Stop Procrastinating and Get More Done in Less Time.*

The Writer's Sandbox – Starting

1. GET CLEAR ON WHAT YOU WANT TO DO

Stop delaying on your goals. If you're feeling stuck, the best way to get started is to go small. This approach works at every stage of your writing life. You might be at the beginning of a project, dancing round your dream trying to find out where to start, or you can apply this as a daily practice of prioritisation, warming up the writing muscles with a quick win to build confidence.

Take a moment to consider what you want to do. It might be an outcome goal like a completed article or chapter, or a practice goal like writing regularly. Do you have a specific goal or project in mind? Is there a behaviour you want to work on, such as writing for a certain amount of time or a number of words or pages?

Name your goal and write it down, before figuring out the best way to approach it.

2. APPROACHES TO IDENTIFYING A FIRST STEP

Take the behaviour or goal you're working on and either scale it back or find a starter step.

Scaling back is great for outcome goals, such as working on a specific project like an article, novel or thesis. Rather than consider the whole thing, scale it back to something small and easily achievable. Don't write 500 pages, write one page, half a page, perhaps even a paragraph.

Starter steps move you towards the behaviour you want to build. They are something very small that gets you familiar with writing – for example, opening your notebook or naming a document. At the very beginning it's not even about doing any writing: by keeping the bar low you'll start a routine and be able to keep it alive.

At this stage the step should be small. The point is to get you off the starting blocks; once you're feeling comfortable you can increase. But for now, think super small to bypass the fear centres of your brain. If you start to feel worried or panicky, that's a sign you need to go smaller.

3. BRAINSTORM

You are more likely to have a successful idea if you've got a choice of ideas.[23]

Grab a piece of paper and write your goal in the centre of the page. Then go wild and free-form as you note down all the things that could help you achieve it – these could be steps to take immediately, they could be things you need to stop doing to make time for writing. Have fun with this exercise and get out of your comfort zone.

Finally, select one that is easy, quick or fun to do.

 Our writing goals planner helps you name your dream, make it SMART and identify a first step. To download it, go to: **prolifiko. com/writtenresources**

4. BUILD IT UP

You might be rather sceptical about the small-steps approach, and of course it will take forever to write a 70,000-word book if you are only writing ten words a day.*

However, if you consistently show up and do your small step, you'll become familiar with it, less scared, and also better at it. That's when you increase the step into something larger.

Turn up each session, repeat, and the behaviour will build without freaking out your amygdala.

5. FIND A PROMPT TO EMBED THE BEHAVIOUR

Prompts will anchor your step into your day. Identify an existing routine (like brushing your teeth or eating your breakfast) or an event (like a phone notification) that can act as a cue to remind you to do the new behaviour. Experiment with which prompts works best for you.

---

* Forever in this case is 7,000 days or 19.18 years.

6. FEEL GOOD ABOUT YOUR PROGRESS

Throughout this chapter we've talked about how motivation is a fickle and unreliable friend for writers; that doesn't mean writing should be miserable. In fact, feeling good about your writing will help you keep going, especially when you hit hard times.

Notice each time you take a step or reach a milestone. Embed that positive feeling by tapping into your brain's reward circuitry with a celebration, reward or treat – these will help you recognise progress and lead to feelings of success as your project moves forward, step by step.

FAST   SLOW

AUTOPILOT ATTENTION

SYSTEM 1 + SYSTEM 2

CHAPTER 6

OBSTACLE THINKING

6

STOPPING

Manage daily distractions with
a plan of action (not an iron will)

B ack in 2009, celebrated writer Neil Gaiman was replying to a fan who'd contacted him through his blog. Gareth wanted some advice. He was disappointed that George R.R. Martin, author of the massively successful TV smash *Game of Thrones*, hadn't yet delivered on the next instalment of his *A Song of Ice and Fire* novel series on which the show is based. 'I've become increasingly frustrated with Martin's lack of communication on the next novel's publication date,' complained Gareth. 'It's almost as though he is doing everything in his power to avoid working on it... Is it unrealistic to think that by not writing the next chapter Martin is letting me down?' In Gaiman's response, titled 'Entitlement Issues', he wrote: 'This may not be palatable, Gareth, and I keep trying to come up with a better way to put it, but the simplicity of things, at least from my perspective is this: *George R.R. Martin is not your bitch.* This is a useful thing to know, perhaps a useful thing to point out when you find yourself thinking that possibly George is, indeed, your bitch, and should be out there typing what you want to read *right now*. People are not machines. Writers and artists aren't machines.'[1]

EVERYONE BOTHERS ME EVERY DAY

It's true that *The Winds of Winter*, the sixth novel in Martin's series, was due to be delivered by 2014 (as it's now 2023 Gareth must be at boiling point). The author appears to still be working on an early draft. In an interview, a friend and collaborator attempted an explanation, saying that *Game of Thrones* has been something of a double-edged sword.[2] Yes, it's been a global phenomenon, but that success has left the writer with much to distract him and an ever-dwindling attention span. At the time of writing, Martin is busying himself with all sorts of projects including new *Game of Thrones* prequels, sequels and spin-offs – but not, it would appear, the long-awaited sixth book. His life is now bursting with exciting alternatives – but these come with a cost. 'Because the books and the show are so popular, I have interviews to do constantly. I have travel plans constantly,' he admitted at a conference.[3] 'It's like suddenly I get invited to travel to South Africa or Dubai, and who's passing up a free trip to Dubai?' Exciting opportunities indeed, but ones that lead to delay, as Martin explains: 'I don't write when I travel. I don't write in hotel rooms. I don't write on airplanes. I really have to be in my own house undisturbed to write. Through most of my life nobody did bother me, but now everyone bothers me every day.' Martin's current radical solution is to move lock, stock and barrel to an isolated hilltop writing cabin at an undisclosed location. Ably helped by a small army of minions (his word), Martin's every need is catered for and every potential writing distraction, interruption or mild irritation is deftly, silently removed by a minion before it ever disturbs him. There, Martin complains his life is very boring, 'Truth be told, I hardly can be said to have a life,' he writes on his blog.[4] But at least he is able to focus on the writing. Let's hope it helps.

This serves as a healthy reminder: even the world's most successful, experienced, wealthy, talented and celebrated writers are human. They get distracted and interrupted – just like everyone else. They have doubts and fears – just like everyone else. Some might say they make excuses to avoid writing – as we do too. In this chapter, we'll consider what's going on in your brain when you get distracted and how a subtle shift of approach can give you more time and focus than you thought you had. We'll also explore some practical methods to keep you focussed and motivated when you feel your writing life is full of obstacles.

● ● ●

We run writing sprints to help writers to keep going. These are week-long programmes designed to get people off the starting blocks and give them a friendly shove in the right direction. As part of these, writers spill the beans on the kinds of things that distract them day to day. We've been running sprints for a few years now, so this has given us quite an insight into the daily struggles people have. We analysed a sample of 500 writers – what obstacles do you think come top?

You might not be too surprised to hear that work interruptions crop up in over half of all responses (54 per cent), while 20 per cent of writers say that their phone distracts them. For 16 per cent of writers, social media platforms are to blame (with one in particular – Facebook), and 10 per cent say the urge to check news headlines is the thing that pulls them away the most. Domestic life features highly too. Household chores stop 9 per cent from writing, while 16 per cent say their family is principally responsible for distracting them (with husbands more distracting than wives, and daughters more distracting than sons – the reasons why are perhaps the subject for another book). The other category of writing distractions named were more emotional in nature – something we'll address in the next chapter. For 29 per cent of writers, interruptions like fear, overwhelm, anxiety, perfectionism and loss of confidence are significant enough to stop them.*

While many writers blame themselves for getting pulled away by distractions like these, they shouldn't be so hard on themselves. The Nobel Prize-winning psychologist Daniel Kahneman explains that getting distracted is just human nature. We can select and choose what to attend to, but we're also involuntarily drawn to certain things because of our brain's wiring. He writes: 'The sophisticated allocation of attention has been honed by a long history of evolutionary history. Orienting and responding quickly to the gravest threats or most promising opportunities improved the chance of survival.'[5]

THE EFFORT OF PAYING ATTENTION

Over a lifetime of research, Kahneman developed the influential theory that our brains process the world in two modes – fast and slow. In 'fast' processing mode, or what he calls System 1, we process the world on autopilot. This system is quick, subconscious and always on. For example, we don't have to 'think' what the answer to 2 + 2 is, and we instinctively whip our heads round when we're startled by a loud noise. System 2 processing, on the other hand, is slower and requires more cognitive effort. It's difficult, if not impossible, to multitask when we're processing in slow mode. It's why we might stop what we're doing when we get asked a difficult question. It's the reason why we might want to write in silence or why libraries and exam halls tend to be quiet.

In his book *Thinking, Fast and Slow*, Kahneman gives an example of Systems 1 and 2 in action, which we're embellishing a

---

* Writers on the sprint were able to list more than just one distraction (life is very distracting after all), which explains why the percentages go above 100.

little here. Imagine it's a sunny day and you're the passenger in a car whizzing along an open freeway. You're happily gossiping with the driver who's got one eye on the road. But then your driver takes a wrong turn. Suddenly, you're driving on a narrow clifftop trail with vertical drops – the rain has started lashing down too. Now, your driver must undertake a complicated manoeuvre and overtake a truck on a blind corner. What's the first thing you'd do? That's right, you'd probably stop talking sharpish and cling on for dear life. Why? Because we know instinctively that the driver needs to pay attention to the road and that talking to her might be distracting. We know that the driver can't easily process multiple stimuli anymore, so we limit their cognitive input because we want her to focus.

Tasks that are complicated like this 'take' more of our limited attention spans than others because they involve more mental effort. Writing is also one of these tasks. In fact, Kahneman refers to writing as an 'optimal experience'[6] – an activity which places high demands on our System 2 processing powers. While you might be able to have some music on in the background when you're writing, you might struggle to write and solve a complicated maths equation at the same time. Writing is effortful because it involves discipline, self-control and having to concentrate hard.

In the same way that we have evolved to protect ourselves against risk or stress,* Kahneman explains that we've also evolved to avoid anything that taxes us too much – either mentally or physically. He calls the System 2 part of the brain the 'lazy controller', in that it's always looking for a simple and untaxing way to do things. Procrastination occurs because our brains are trying to protect us

---

* If you remember from Chapter 5, setting small, achievable goals and moving forward in small, realistic steps works because it tiptoes past the fear centres in your brain which can be triggered when you take on too much.

from overexertion. Something even Nobel Prize-winning scientists are prone to do: 'An observer of the number of times I look at email, or investigate the refrigerator during an hour of writing could reasonably confer an urge to escape and conclude that keeping at it requires more self-control than I can readily muster,' writes Kahneman.[7]

While the 'threats' that break our concentration today might come in the shape of a smartphone rather than a sabre-toothed tiger, they are far more abundant. Being able to concentrate when necessary so that we are not living our lives 'in the shallows', as writer Nicholas Carr puts it, is a vital skill.[8] It's clear that the big choices we make in our life about what to pay attention to and focus on – relationship A or B, career path X or Y – have a profound and important impact on our lives. However, the smaller-scale choices we make, like whether we write for 30 minutes before the kids wake up, matter too. In many ways, much more. It's important that we pay attention to these because all these small choices add up. As science writer Winifred Gallagher neatly explains, 'Deciding what to pay attention to for this hour, day, week, or year, much less a lifetime is a deeply human predicament and your quality of life largely depends on how you handle it.'[9] So, while it's important to recognise that distraction is natural, that's not to say we shouldn't try to keep focussed.

It's hard to write with constant interruptions, but equally hard if there are no consequences, no stakes, no deadlines to meet and nobody to disappoint (aside from yourself) or millions of eager fans to potentially disappoint (perhaps at the root of George R.R. Martin's delay). Over the years working with a wide variety of writers, we've learned that the amount of time you have at your disposal and the number of distractions you have in your life do not in themselves stifle your concentration or allow you to focus. In short, you can write with a lot of time or a little, with many interruptions and distractions or few – often, it comes down to you and the approach you take.

Behavioural economist Paul Dolan explains that when you get distracted you experience a kind of mental friction, or what he refers to as 'switching costs'.* Flitting between projects and never focussing deeply on one can be deeply damaging, because it means we never achieve a sense of flow – that feeling of being completely absorbed in a task.† As we've learned, we have only a finite amount of System 2 processing power that we can give to things during a given day, so it's best to use it wisely. Every time we're distracted by a tweet, our reserves our depleted. Research shows that simply reading a piece of text online with multiple embedded links is more mentally tiring that reading the same text without the links. This is because each link presents a micro decision. Should it be opened or not? And little by little, this chips away at our reserves.[10]

Dolan explains how damaging it can be to our productivity and our overall happiness levels when we are forced away from the thing we want to concentrate on against our will. 'Every time you shift your attention, your brain has to re-orientate itself, further taxing your mental resources. When you respond to a text, tweet, or email, you are using attentional energy to switch tasks. If you do

---

* It is not clear where the origin for the term 'switching costs' comes from, although Dolan references a study from 2000 by Meiran, Chorev and Sapir, 'Component processes in task switching', which might be the original source.

† The concept of 'flow' was coined by the psychologist Mihály Csíkszentmihályi in 1975 and is explained comprehensively in his book from 1990 of the same name. In it, he defines flow as the way people describe their state of mind when consciousness is harmoniously ordered and they want to pursue whatever they are doing for its own sake. He goes on to outline how flow is fundamental to achieving a sense of happiness and fulfilment in our lives. His research also explains how being denied flow can be damaging to both our mental health and wellbeing.

this frequently, your attention reserves become quickly diminished, making it harder for you to focus on whatever you want to do.'[11]

Distractions are damaging because they're intrusive and out of our control. The more we can bring them under our control, the less damaging they become. When you think about it, the only difference between a distraction that takes our concentration away from the writing and a break that we deliberately plan into our day is our mindset. One 'happens to us', the other we do intentionally. The break we choose to take involves a free and autonomous choice and therefore less cognitive effort. The break we're forced to take gives our brains more friction and stress. This means that the more control you have over your distractions, the less effort you'll expend and the happier and more contented your brain will be. As we've said, your brain always wants to find an easy way out – the next two approaches will help you turn your brain's natural laziness to your advantage.

OBSTACLE THINKING

In an interview, the psychologist Gabriele Oettingen explained why she became interested in the science of goal-setting and motivation – a field in which she's a world-leading authority: 'I was always interested in hope,' she says. 'Why people don't give up despite the most dire circumstances. At first, I thought it was positive thinking. But then we learned from the data that it's not that simple. Positive thinking is great for exploring possibilities about the future. It's also good for your mood. But when it comes to attaining your desired future – then it's a real detriment. What we really need is action – so that people can change their lives. Positive fantasies about the future are not the answer to how people are resilient. Positive daydreams about the future must be complemented with a sound sense of reality.'[12]

Her research finds that positive, hopeful thinking can give you direction but it must be paired with something more practical: you need to know what's standing in your way. When you try to keep focussed through willpower alone – the 'fight your distractions' approach – you're not only depleting your cognitive energy, you're also relying on a hope and a dream that things will change in the future. You're wishing that something will turn out better than it did last time, without knowing why you struggled to focus in the first place.

Oettingen observed people of different ages and in different contexts for over twenty years to understand whether having positive fantasies of the future would lead to improved motivation to act. She ran experiments on people wanting to achieve all kinds of goals – from losing weight or finding a new job to quitting smoking. Her research took before and after measurements of subjects' systolic blood pressure – a cardiovascular measure revealing how energised or motivated a person is. She found that whatever goal we want to attain, daydreaming about that goal calms us and reduces our blood pressure. 'It's remarkable that positive fantasies help us relax to such an extent that it shows up in physiological tests,' she writes.[13]

Of course, in today's non-stop world there's nothing wrong with a spot of daydreaming – in fact, you may recall we examined the benefits earlier. But the problem that Oettingen finds is that having positive fantasies leads you to feel chilled out, and when you're in that state you're less likely to do anything. If you want to meet your goals, 'the *last* thing you want to be is relaxed', she writes. 'You want to be energised enough to get off the couch and lose those pounds or find that job or study for that test, and you want to be motivated enough to stay engaged even when the inevitable obstacles or challenges arise.'[14] So yes, by all means daydream, but don't stop there. To repeat what Booker Prize-winning novelist

Bernardine Evaristo said, 'manifestations don't work if you don't do the work'. Having dreams might make you feel warm and fuzzy – but it doesn't lead to you taking action, which of course is the only way you'll make them a reality.

When thinking about whatever goal we want to reach in any area of our lives, Oettingen suggests we use a process called 'mental contrasting' – have your dream but then visualise some of the personal barriers and impediments that might stop you from achieving that dream. This mental contrasting approach, or as we call it 'obstacle thinking', is something we use to start every coaching programme. We ask writers to name the kinds of distractions and interruptions they may encounter over the course of their time working with us. The approach might help you too.

It's powerful because it helps you think through the things that might stop you writing and so enables you to manage them better when you experience them. Rather than wait for distractions to disturb you, obstacle thinking helps you predict your interruptions. And this means that you're no longer expelling cognitive effort 'trying' to keep focussed. When you use it, you turn a hopeful thought such as: *If only my dog would stop coming into my room in the afternoon and annoying me with her squeaky toy*, into practical action instead, like: *I'm going to walk my dog at 3pm so she's tired and I'll put the darned squeaky toy on a shelf – sorry, Peggy.*

It's motivating to have a positive vision of the future, like a finished manuscript or book. However, that dream must be accompanied with a sound understanding of what might stop you from getting there and a knowledge of what to do when you do hit a bump in the road – which you inevitably will. This method isn't necessarily about achieving some sort of distraction-free writing bliss; rather it's about giving the System 2 part of your brain less to do. When you become more mindful of the interruptions that might occur during the course of your day (or indeed your life), you also become better able to dodge them when they happen. By getting ahead of your distractions, you're minimising the cognitive load that comes along with involuntarily being taken away from the writing. You're avoiding the kind of switching costs we learned about from Dolan. But what if your distractions were removed entirely?

CHOICE ARCHITECTURE

When success came to the poet, memoirist and civil rights activist Maya Angelou, she did not complicate her life with exciting things to do and then move to a hill-top retreat in order to escape them. Rather, she kept to her routine and designed her writing life to be simpler. In an interview, she said that her day started early – around six in the morning. After a coffee with her husband, she left for her workplace: a hotel room which she'd deliberately stripped of any distractions. 'I keep a hotel room in which I do my work,' she said in another interview, 'a tiny, mean room with just a bed, and some-times, if I can find it, a face basin.' She had no need of assistants to keep her focussed, she did this herself by restricting what she took into the room. If it was today, she'd certainly leave her phone at home and cut the wifi to her laptop. She said: 'I keep a diction-ary, a Bible, a deck of cards and a bottle of sherry in the room. It's lonely, and it's marvellous.'[15] What Angelou was doing – not that she would have described it as such – was using the principles of environment design to keep her focussed. As we touched on ear-lier, our attention is finite. It's why we talk about focus in the same way we talk about money. We 'pay' attention to such and such, we 'invest' time in something.

The idea that we can deliberately impact our behaviour – the choices and decisions we make – by how we arrange the things in our lives was popularised by behavioural scientist and economist

Richard Thaler* with journalist Cass Sunstein. Their simple but powerful idea – choice architecture – is that we can change how we act by reducing the number of choices we have to make. You can make it easier to write, for example, by reducing or eliminating the distractions that typically pull you away. It's a theory that's been used by governments across the world to help 'nudge' us to do things that we know in our hearts make sense but don't get round to doing – like getting fit, saving for a pension or getting the winter flu jab. Being interviewed by the *Paris Review*, Angelou explained that there was something about her bare room that brought her the creative focus she needed: 'I go into the room and I feel as if all my beliefs are suspended. Nothing holds me to anything.'[16] She also said there was something about her home environment which meant she struggled to focus: 'I try to keep home very pretty and I can't work in a pretty surrounding – it throws me.'[17] Angelou knew that in order to write, she needed to arrange her writing environment in a way that kept her limited System 2 attention on the work. Indeed, she even asked the hotel staff to take the pictures down from the walls of her room so she could keep her attention on the writing and nothing else.

The approaches we've considered so far are about managing and knowing how to respond to the daily interruptions you face, rather than fighting them with an iron will. Both of these approaches remove or reduce the number of stressful things your brain needs to do and therefore makes focussing easier. But there is also a way we can harness our natural desire for what the eminent psychologist

---

* Thaler spent a year at Stanford University between 1977 and 1978 working with Daniel Kahneman and Amos Tversky (with whom Kahneman jointly developed the Systems 1 and 2 theory). Kahneman and Tversky's work provided him with a theoretical framework to explain many of the economic anomalies he was researching at the time.

Robert Cialdini calls 'cognitive closure'. It helps us keep motivated and makes it easy to return to writing the next day – try it yourself, your lazy brain will thank you again.

HARNESSING OPEN LOOPS

One day early on his career, Cialdini was coming to the end of one of his lectures when he suddenly noticed that he'd run out of time. He'd have to finish his talk without giving the students the answer to the meaty question he'd posed at the beginning. At the time, Cialdini thought nothing of it. He wound up the class with a brief apology and said he'd give them the answer next time. But they didn't want to go away. He'd left them hanging with an open loop. They wanted to find out what the answer to the question was. 'They would not let me stop until I had given them closure on the mystery. I remember thinking, "Cialdini, you've stumbled onto dynamite here!"' [18]

He knew it was a breakthrough moment but he still didn't know what had just happened. So, he started researching different psychological theories and discovered that it was something to do with a recognised 'state' called the Zeigarnik effect. He describes in his book *Pre-suasion* how the Zeigarnik effect was first discovered. We'll retell the story for you now. One day, a group of students and research assistants were lazing around in a sunny beer garden in 1920s Berlin when talk turned to a veteran waiter who worked there. The waiter was famous far and wide for his amazing ability to perfectly memorise the orders of huge tables of people and accurately distribute the right food and drink orders every time.

One of the students decided to test the limits of the elderly waiter's memory, so after he'd delivered another large order she asked her fellow students to all cover their plates with napkins. She then asked the waiter to return. Then, she asked him to tell her again who had ordered what dish. The waiter peered at the students he'd served just minutes before and at the table now strewn with napkins – but he couldn't do it. He couldn't even come close. This sounds like a cheeky student question until you understand that it was in fact part of a study led by Kurt Lewin, the father of modern social psychology, and Bluma Zeigarnik, a napkin-wielding Lithuanian research psychologist who went on to be a world-renowned expert in memory.

The Zeigarnik effect is a state which means that people remember uncompleted or interrupted tasks better than completed ones, because our attention is drawn to them. Cialdini thinks it's all to do with our innate craving for what he calls 'cognitive closure'. When the waiter was in the midst of a task, his memory was second to none – all his mental energy was on that task. But once that order was completed and that loop had been closed, he'd mentally moved on. 'On a task that we feel committed to performing, we will remember all sorts of elements of it better if we have not yet had the chance to finish, because our attention will remain drawn to it. If we are engaged in such a task and are interrupted or pulled away, we'll feel a discomforting, gnawing desire to get back to it.'[19]

Cialdini says that he harnesses the Zeigarnik effect himself in that he deliberately finishes writing before he's ready. Finishing early, in mid-sentence and when you really want to keep going – is a tactic writers can use to help them keep focussed so they come back to the writing feeling motivated, knowing what to write next. Ernest Hemingway[20] swore by this approach. And just like Dolan's method we heard about earlier, it involves taking control of what you attend to before you're interrupted and taken away.

● ● ●

'The really important thing about habits and habit change,' said writer and journalist Oliver Burkeman when we interviewed him for our blog, 'is getting back on the horse when you've fallen off rather than never falling off.'[21] What Burkeman is saying here is rather profound – although he's too modest to say that himself.

To extend this equestrian analogy a little further, much like a good horse rider knows the right way to fall to prevent injury (it's to let go of the horse, if you were wondering), you should accept that at some point you will get distracted and interrupted. The key is to know how to respond when these distractions occur rather than dig in and assume they won't happen or 'try harder' to fight them when they do. Both of these responses will only lead to frustration and delay.

When you know what your distractions are and where they come from, you'll be better prepared to manage them, which in turn, means they will have less of an impact on you and your life.

WHEN DISTRACTIONS GO DEEP

This chapter has considered the kinds of daily distractions that keep us from writing – the kind that all of us (George R.R. Martin included) struggle to keep at bay. But many of us experience interruptions of a different order. Often, these interruptions are more internal in nature and they're far more difficult to manage. They are the whisperings of our inner critic. They are the doubts, fears, anxieties and insecurities we all have. These internal thoughts are often what make us more distractable and they can't always be neatly solved with a productivity tip of some kind. In order to address them, you'll need a different approach: one that gives you the resilience you need to keep going when times are tough. And that's what the next chapter is all about.

The Writer's Sandbox – Stopping

1. HOW TO PRACTISE OBSTACLE THINKING

Distractions are everywhere. Email, social media, work, other people – life! It can feel like a constant struggle to manage them. The key to combatting these distractions so they become less disruptive is to understand what they are and where they come from.

First, consider how you get distracted.

Grab a pen or open your laptop. Think back to your last writing session. Make a list of the things that pull you away from your writing. Be as precise as you can, first focussing on a recent and specific time and place – then open out to typical distractions.

- Do you have anything specific that distracts and interrupts you?
- Are there any regular, reoccurring things that pull you away?
- Now, think forward to your next writing session. What might disturb you?
- Is this something that disturbs you all the time or might it be something new?

Think as broadly as possible. You might have many distractions or a few – that's fine. This is not an opportunity to feel bad, but rather to create a realistic map of your distraction tendencies.

2. DESIGN A DISTRACTION-FREE WRITING ENVIRONMENT

We learned earlier that author Maya Angelou wrote from a 'tiny, mean room' to avoid her distractions. While you don't need to go quite as far as that, you can use the principles of choice architecture – a technique from Nobel Prize-winning behavioural scientist Richard Thaler – to keep your focus. In the same way that diabetics reduce the temptation of snacking by hiding sugary treats from view, you can keep your distractions at bay by making a few alterations to where you write.

Once again, this approach all starts with noticing. If you've started a 'distractions log', think about how you can design your environment to remove some of these distractions. For example:

- If you get distracted by email, could you put your phone away in another room or turn off notifications when you write?
- If you get distracted by new ideas, could you quickly capture the idea in some way and get back to the task at hand?
- If you get distracted by an untidy desk or house, could you organise your workspace before you get down to writing?
- If you get distracted by the last thing you wrote, could you try starting on a blank page?

Develop as many practical ideas as you can. It's important to think widely – don't close off ideas.

 Our Distraction Battle Plan will help you identify what gets in the way of your writing and put in place a plan of action. To download it, go to: **prolifiko.com/writtenresources**

3. HOW TO TAKE BACK CONTROL OF YOUR ATTENTION

The better able we are to take control of the distractions we have day-to-day, the better we can manage them. Start by using breaks intentionally.

Now you know some of your distraction tendencies, think about how you can plan these into your writing day. Instead of waiting for these distractions to pull your attention away and cause the kind of switching costs we learned about from behavioural economist Paul Dolan, it's time to take a more intentional, proactive approach. For example:

- If you notice that you start to get distracted after writing for a certain amount of time, this could be a signal that you need to step away.

- Reflect on when you start to get distracted and schedule in a short break to do something else. Go outside, grab a coffee, step away from your desk, clear your head in some way.

4. USE YOUR DISTRACTIONS AS REWARDS

A second approach to take back control is to harness your distractions. When you procrastinate from the writing, it's likely that you'll end up doing something less stressful instead. However, now you know what some of your typical distractions are, you can turn them to your advantage by using them as little rewards for a writing session. For example:

- If you've noticed that Instagram is the thing that you get distracted by, reward yourself with a 10-minute Insta binge – but only after you've done some writing.
- If you find yourself drifting off to research yet another gadget online when you should be writing, instead make time to 'research' at the end of the day once the writing is done.

The principle here is not to deny yourself these little pleasures throughout the day, but rather to incorporate them into your writing process so they become motivators.

5. HARNESS THE POWER OF OPEN LOOPS

Remember Robert Cialdini's revelation from his early days of teaching? He found that he could keep his students engaged by giving them a cliffhanger at the end of a lecture. The brain craves cognitive closure and dislikes open loops – but you can turn that to your advantage by deliberately stopping writing before you are ready.

This is a super-simple but highly effective method. The key is not to close the loop. When you're on a roll, step away from the writing before you're ready – literally, mid-sentence. It keeps your brain ticking over and can mean you're more motivated to get going when you return to...

Part Three

KEEP WRITING

What five things would you tell an aspiring author?

1. *Write a lot.*
2. *Find what you like writing.*
3. *Write it a lot.*
4. *Find someone who publishes writing like yours.*
5. *Keep writing even if everyone hates it.*

– David Quantick*

---

* David Quantick is an Emmy Award-winning comedy writer, best-selling author and music journalist. He works regularly with writer and director Armando Iannucci on shows such as *Avenue 5*, *The Thick of It* and *Veep*, and his books include *The Mule*, *How to Write Everything* and *How to Be a Writer*.

KINDNESS

SMALL STEPS

CHAPTER 7

 VS

COMPARISON

 WHAT IF...?

BREAKING NEWS

SHIT HAPPENS

7

RESILIENCE

When big things happen,
it's the small things that keep you going

Imagine that one day your fairy godmother flew down from wherever fairy godmothers live, waved her sparkly wand, and granted you all the space, time and money you needed to write. Would you shower her with thanks and jump for joy or would you, like Professor Abigail Harrison Moore, react rather differently? For years, Harrison Moore had wanted to write a monograph. She'd done the research, sketched out a rough plan – but she never had time. One day she received a message from her faculty awarding her a year's research leave on full pay to write it. You might think she'd be overjoyed, but her response was: 'I can't do it.' A few weeks later, when she received another message that her sabbatical had been postponed for a year because of the COVID-19 pandemic, she thought, *Thank God!*

It would be an understatement to say that many of us have a tricky relationship with writing. Often, it's the thing that we desperately want to do, but it's also the thing that we stop doing – or indeed, never start. When something is hard and contains more mental effort, we're more likely to delay, get distracted and kick the can down the road. Which is what Harrison Moore's first instinct was. We mentioned earlier that there's something about the creative process that makes writing hard and rewarding in equal measure.

That means we need resilience to continue writing when things get tough. This chapter tells the stories of two very different writers who, for their own personal reasons, stopped writing. We'll explore how they got writing again and what we can learn about how to keep going.

● ● ●

It takes persistence to build an academic career. Harrison Moore has clocked up 28 years in academia; she's a senior professor, was until recently the head of a large department at her university, and is an expert in her field of Art History and Museum Studies. Despite all this, Harrison Moore told us that she feels like an imposter. 'I often think to myself – how did I end up here? It wasn't meant to happen. I'm a state schoolgirl from Yorkshire who got lucky,' she said. 'I know it's ridiculous, but sometimes I feel like a fraud.'

Harrison Moore came into academia to teach – research and writing was far from her mind. 'I see myself as an educator and a communicator first and foremost, but then I was told that you have to be this thing called "an academic", you have to write books and get published too.' Her colleagues put pressure on her to write, otherwise her career would suffer. That's how the scholarly system works: academic writers are rewarded for being productive. Those who fail to publish are punished, hence the brutal 'publish or perish' message drummed into early-career researchers. She explains: 'Writing became an obligation – something I had to do. Something I never really enjoyed.' Negative remarks from supervisors and senior colleagues early on didn't help. 'When I started out, people told me that I wasn't a proper researcher – that it was my job to look after the students and stick to the spreadsheets. I'm mostly over those comments, but it's still there deep inside.' She confesses that the pressure to write, publish and 'be an academic' had even led her to consider leaving academia altogether some years ago.* The promotion to head of school recognised her strengths and meant she stuck with it, but the new responsibilities took her further away from research and writing and left her with even less time.

THE ORDINARY MAGIC OF RESILIENCE

Resilience is considered a panacea. Often described as a personality trait, it enables us to survive in the short term and thrive in the long term. Coming from the Latin *resilire* 'to rebound', it's the ability to bounce back. In engineering, the most resilient materials are not the strongest ones, but rather the flexible ones that are able to respond to shocks. Being resilient is not about toughing it out, nor does it stop difficult things from happening, but the promise of resilience is that it helps us to recover from difficulties and adapt in response to adversity rather than give up. As well as the struggles that go along with writing, like dealing with blocks, negative feedback and rejection, we build resilience in the face of life's knock-backs – illness, money worries, family problems, grief and trauma, and for some of us, all of these things in quick succession. So, how do we develop more of it?

---

* We'll hear how Harrison Moore developed tactics to deal with the pressure she experienced. But while she managed that, many don't. It important to note that resilience isn't always an option for academics. In the UK, 30 per cent of people who start PhDs drop out, while in the USA the attrition rate is 50 per cent. Those with full-time jobs or who study part-time are more likely to drop out.[1] For many, working while studying is not a choice but a financial imperative; those without money are set up to fail. When one UK university looked at barriers to doctoral education it found: 'Financial factors, which restrict students' educational choices, present one of the most challenging obstacles to accessing doctoral education.' Bundled under non-financial factors, it found that women, Black British students, and those with disabilities experience persistent challenges which influenced PhD completion and their post-doctoral career progression.[2]

Ann S. Masten is an internationally known expert on resilience in human development who has dedicated her career to researching how individuals can survive and adapt despite the most adverse circumstances. While reviewing the findings of longitudinal studies of children who overcome adversity, she had a surprising, but counter-intuitive, breakthrough. Rather than discovering that resilient individuals were possessed of extraordinary talents and skills, the evidence showed that resilience is common. Masten's thesis is a simple one: 'Resilience arises from "ordinary magic" and it is possible to understand where it comes from and how to foster it.' She provides an optimistic perspective and a practical framework that makes resilience possible.[3] Let's look at what this means for our blocked professor.

What stopped Harrison Moore from the writing wasn't a lack of enthusiasm or a lack of knowledge – passion for her subject and for her students brims over when we talk. It was something else. 'I know what I want to say. Put me in front of a room of people and I can stand up and talk for ages – but put me in front of a keyboard and I start to lose confidence.' While Harrison Moore wasn't blocked to the extent she couldn't write anything – she was a successful professor after all – the process of writing was making her unhappy.

She wanted to get back a sense of balance and enjoyment, and to stop delaying and fearing the process. She had proven she could write and get published; her first monograph, published in 2011, grew 'almost organically' out of a footnote in her PhD that intrigued her and inspired a connection. She was able to explore ideas, get lost down rabbit holes and be creative. That book was the last thing she'd enjoyed writing on her own, a decade ago. Over her academic career she'd built up baggage; for years she only listened to the negative voices, both her own and others. Writing had become associated with work, career and obligation.

We encouraged her to keep a writing diary, a place where she could consider what she enjoyed, and didn't enjoy, about the writing process. Exploring those reflections in coaching calls gave her insight; she realised that she'd internalised myths about how academics should write and what she, as an academic, should be able to achieve. 'Telling myself to sit down to write for two hours and write 1,000 words feels intimidating because I feel obligated about the end result,' said Harrison Moore. 'So now, I take the approach of taking a word and playing around with it, perhaps doing some freewriting, taking a quote from an archive and exploring what it means.' Instead of giving herself output-driven writing goals to complete – like 'write the conclusion' or 'write 2,000 words' – she allowed herself time to be more playful.

What Harrison Moore started to do was to lower the stakes and make small changes that connected her to the process of writing. She stopped forcing herself to write using willpower alone and jettisoned the approaches that hadn't worked in the past. She slowly released the pressure valve and took the expectation away. Writing had become a burden; something she had to do for her career rather than something she enjoyed and did well. She also stopped embarking on lengthy writing sessions – something that she believed she should be able to do as an academic – and wrote just a small amount every day. 'For my whole career I've always believed that the only way I'll ever write is in long periods of time – otherwise there's no point in starting. But I've come to realise that's just wrong.' Once she started to note down her reflections and check in with her writing each day, the inner critic who used to whisper: 'You're not an academic, you shouldn't be here' was silenced. Writing the book became less of a big deal.

When the time came for her postponed research leave to start, she didn't curse, delay or kick it further down the road. During her sabbatical Harrison Moore wrote a journal article and two large research grants, published one edited collection, and is well on the way with the promised monograph. With every word she writes, with each essay, grant and book she contributes to, with every invitation she accepts, the feeling of being a fraud fades. The negative voices – both her own and others – are counterbalanced with evidence that she is a writer.

● ● ●

While writing this book we spoke to writers who have faced a myriad of challenges such as getting stuck, losing confidence when their book is rejected by an agent or they aren't published, not hitting the sales target, not being read, reviewed or cited, or facing criticism and abuse. We spoke to writers dealing with the death of a co-author or a family member, those who face ongoing struggles like long-term illness or recurring mental health issues. One thing struck us from all these conversations: when you face big challenges, you need to go small.

The advice to go small feels illogical, plain wrong, or at worst completely trite. When we suffer big challenges we think we need big solutions, ones that require Herculean efforts. Yet, like Harrison Moore and her decision to be more playful with her writing, it's the ease of the solution that makes it achievable and therefore a powerful enabler of change. To explore this, we're going to meet someone determined to keep writing under the most extreme circumstances. We're sharing this story because resilience is a process; it can be developed and we can survive – and keep writing. We hope it inspires you to keep going.

After nine years of research, Shireen Jeejeebhoy was on a roll with her non-fiction book. She'd dealt with a whole series of writing obstacles – from getting to grips with technical research to the loss of an agent and the drama of securing funding for the project – but none of that prepared her for the battle to come. When a car accident left her unable to read or write, it took immense resilience to manage her injuries and keep writing.

After the accident, Jeejeebhoy's medical team swung into action. Their primary focus was fixing the physical injuries to her shoulder and arm, so even though she'd suffered whiplash, brain injury wasn't considered for four months. A psychologist suggested an electroencephalography (EEG) test, where an electrode attached to her scalp signalled that her brainwaves were low. It took another five months to get a specialist scan and a formal diagnosis of brain injury. That was just the beginning. While Jeejeebhoy was undergoing intensive neurorehabilitation and learning to write again, as reactive fibromyalgia triggered pain all over her body, she found herself in the courts fighting her insurance companies in not one but two lawsuits lasting eight and half years.

HOW TO BUILD RESILIENCE

While Jeejeebhoy credits 'good old-fashioned bloody-mindedness' for helping her to get through, being resilient is not about an individual toughing it out. As resilience researcher Ann S. Masten explains, the field of resilience studies is dynamic; models and definitions are changing all the time. There's been a shift from seeing resilience as personal adaptation to viewing it as a process that includes systems such family, community, organisations and ecosystems. It's helpful to see resilience as natural human adaptation, in short 'ordinary magic', a dynamic process that draws on different elements. Take the American Psychological Association's (APA) guidance on how we can increase our resilience.[4] It suggests four core components:

1. **Purpose** – being proactive, making progress towards goals, finding opportunities for self-discovery and helping others.
2. **Healthy thinking** – accepting that challenges will happen, learning from past experiences, and maintaining a hopeful outlook that keeps things in perspective and embraces change.
3. **Connection** – this includes strategies such as prioritising relationships and joining a group.
4. **Wellness** – having a healthy body, taking up practices like mindfulness, and avoiding negative outlets like substance abuse.

We can't stop difficult things happening, but the promise of resilience is that we become stronger, more adaptable and better equipped to deal with life's tougher moments. It's not just about dealing with one-off shocks, but an ongoing process between individuals and the communities around them. Let's look at how Jeejeebhoy modelled the components identified by the APA starting with that 'hopeful outlook' under healthy thinking.

In the last chapter we met Gabriele Oettingen who was investigating hope as part of a study on resilience. She found that we need to pair our dreams with a dose of reality, a tactic she calls mental contrasting.[5] The starting point for this is visualising your wish as fully as possible. Oettingen first gets people to imagine their 'dearest wish' and then gets them to visualise the best outcome 'as vividly as possible'. She explains: 'Give your thoughts and imagination free rein. Let your mind go.'[6] This is visualising success, and Oettingen suggests closing our eyes to help us to imagine and feel as fully as we can.*

Jeejeebhoy said: 'For writing, you really need to have a goal, but

---

* All that visualising practice from Chapter 4 should have primed you to have a dream and a goal.

you also need that goal to have meaning for you. If it doesn't have meaning, it's not going be something that will keep you going.' The book she was writing provided that meaning. When her accident happened, Jeejeebhoy was working on a biography of a woman who made medical history as the first person to live for decades at home, solely on intravenous feeding. In 1970 Judy Taylor had suffered intestinal blood clots which annihilated her digestive system. She faced the prospect of starving to death in hospital when she met Dr Khursheed Jeejeebhoy, Shireen's father, a recent immigrant to Toronto who had an innovative idea about how to save her. Writing this book ticks off many of the APA's components for 'purpose': it's a goal that has meaning, and which offers opportunities for self (and family) discovery, and for helping others.

It also taught her about 'healthy thinking' as she learnt from her early writing challenges and gave her opportunities for 'connection'. In 1991 Jeejeebhoy started researching Taylor's story, which involved detailed medical research and upwards of 60 interviews with medical specialists, fellow patients, friends and family. She encountered extreme obstacles: a longed-for New York agent deal collapsing and the car accident which took away her ability to read and write. Jeejeebhoy went from being an avid reader of around 150 books a year to not being able to decipher words and meaning; she used to be able to write 16,000 words per chapter, but even after intensive rehab could now only manage 800 words. Worse than that, her medical team didn't understand her need or desire to write. It took a year and a half to relearn how to write, and over five years before she could put in place the systems that supported her to return to the book project. Her primary focus was getting her health back, but her desire to write and finish her book gave her a specific purpose. Having a community that helped her continue, coupled with the commitment to the people she was writing about, gave her the connection that the APA highlights as a key element of resilience.

Before her accident in 2000, Jeejeebhoy estimated that her first draft would take six, perhaps nine months to complete. Instead it was another seven years, most of which was spent searching for treatment and then figuring out the systems to help her write. In 2007 she finished writing and published *Lifeliner: The Judy Taylor Story*. It took sixteen years in total to research and write. Since then, she has written and published five non-fiction books, nine novels (several under a pseudonym), has a regular column for *Psychology Today* and manages a writing/publishing business. She also bakes a mighty fine cookie, but before we get to the sweet stuff, we've fallen into a trap that often happens when talking about resilience.

We've heard that in the long term, resilience can lead to growth – even after significant trauma – and can help you improve your life. It's the classic 'triumph over adversity' narrative arc we've been fed through centuries of storytelling. Therein lies the problem. The story of resilience is often based on personal responsibility; that it is up to the individual to manage and move past life's inevitable difficulties. However, putting the onus on the shoulders of individuals sets us up to fail. It took a community for Jeejeebhoy to create the systems she needed to keep going, as well as time and money, and it's not over yet.

DON'T POWER THROUGH

Managing trauma like a brain injury is an ongoing process of resilience. Jeejeebhoy talks about the exhaustion of battling this every day for over twenty years: 'We really need a brand-new word to describe the fatigue from brain injury. It's like you can't keep going. It's not like pain. You can power through pain to a certain extent. But you can't power through fatigue when it hits.'

Over the years, she has pulled together what the APA would call 'wellness' strategies. These range from treating herself to a latte and a chocolate cookie* to supporting other people. When she has a bad day and is feeling low, she goes onto Twitter to 'pump people up'. This activity releases oxytocin which helps her feel good. Again, this is a wonderful combination of the advice to connect with others and to focus on personal self-care. Jeejeebhoy explains: 'You have a certain number of strategies to adjust and to adapt, and think of yourself as a person who's really good at adapting and really good at adjusting.'

While we might not face the same issues as Jeejeebhoy, we can heed her advice to listen to our bodies and their signals. Sometimes, the fact that we get blocked and distracted from our writing is a sign. These don't always need to be managed in some way. Productivity does not mean pressing on regardless. Sometimes – and probably more often than you think – the most productive thing you can do is to stop. Sometimes, stopping should not be resisted, rather it should be embraced. Sometimes you don't need a perky productivity tip to get you going again – you just need to accept that you might be tired. Powering on could lead to burnout. You might be sending yourself a message, so listen to it, be kind to yourself, down tools for a bit, step away from your desk. You'll come back renewed. The following exercises will give you some suggestions on how to tune in to yourself and provide some practical steps to build ordinary magic in your writing life.

---

* Chocolate is often peddled as self-care, but done right it can be helpful, if not essential. Jeejeebhoy's father is a nutritionist and his expert advice to her was: when you have a brain injury, you have to eat. Your brain needs glucose to function, especially if it is working hard. However, the key is to have it *after* cognitive work when the brain is tired. For Jeejeebhoy that means half a home-baked chocolate cookie when she's finished writing.

The Writer's Sandbox – Resilience

1. TUNE IN TO YOUR INTERNAL DISTRACTIONS AND START A 'WORRY DIARY'

Abigail Harrison Moore nearly gave up on writing because of the fear she wasn't a 'proper academic'. Much like the previous chapter where we looked at external distractions, we need to notice what internal beliefs hold us back as writers. That's what this first exercise is all about: the niggling doubts that your writing is not good enough, fears that someone else will have to read the thing you're writing, worries that you'll never finish or won't 'make it' – never get an agent, get published, sell any books.*

Develop a practice of noticing your inner writing critic. In your next writing session, listen to the worries and concerns about your writing that emerge. Observe these thoughts without judgement, then write them down.

Review

At the end of your writing session, read your notes like a scientist would observe results from an experiment. It can be helpful to categorise the whisperings of your writing critic in two ways:

- Practical worries are the type you can take action to address.
- Hypothetical worries are of the 'what if' variety that you can't do much to remedy at the time, such as: 'What if I never get better?'

---

* All writers have these feelings – that said, these exercises are about the *writing* not *the writer*. By that we mean they are primarily designed to deal with thoughts about writing and not negative thoughts about yourself. As with all reflective practice, if doing the exercises in this book makes you feel unduly uncomfortable, you should stop. If the practice uncovers difficult experiences or leads to distressing thoughts, you should seek help and talk to a professional.

Take action

Deal with the practical worries. Go through the list and pick one. Take a moment to explore the worry, but don't ruminate on it. Brainstorm solutions – you might create a mind map or write a list. In general, having multiple ideas for actions to take will lead to better options – then pick one and do it! If it can't be done immediately, schedule it in so you have committed to doing something. If it needs breaking into smaller tasks, do that now, so when you're ready to implement you have a simple route in.

Park the hypothetical

These worries are entirely natural. However, they are damaging because unless you can read minds or own a time machine, they leave you feeling powerless. We've talked to countless writers whose perfectionism and fear of failure at some imagined point in the future has led them to do nothing in the present – and this has impacted their writing and their wellbeing.

If nothing can be done right now to solve these worries – park them. 'Parking' does not mean brushing them under the carpet or dismissing your thoughts as silly. It simply means leaving them to one side for now so they don't derail your progress. Often just acknowledging that you have these fears will help you come to terms with them.

Once parked, they can form a handy editing list when you are further along in the project. Take for example, the thought: *No one will want to read this*. While you are deep in the writing it is often not a good time to share your work, but when you have a completed draft, or an edited and more polished version, you might want to share with trusted readers, editors or coaches. Park that worry and focus on the things you can deal with now.

Spot patterns

Observe your inner writing critic, perhaps noticing what distracting thoughts emerge as you write over a few weeks. We've found that inner writing critics are often lacking in imagination and have a habit of repeating themselves. If you note down what they are say-ing, you might be able to spot patterns. By brainstorming solutions, you'll have some ready-made answers to counter these concerns, backed up with practical steps that are in motion or planned for the future.

Acceptance

This final step is often the toughest for writers: accepting that doubt, fear and uncertainty are part of the creative process and that these feelings will always accompany you. You have to find ways to accept this discomfort and still keep writing.

There is no shortcut to acceptance: it is a process which requires conscious effort to change how you respond to your emotions and adverse situations. If we go back to Harrison Moore, she found that over time she was able to build up evidence that she could write and this counterbalanced the voices (her own and others) that she couldn't. It didn't stop the fear completely, but it helped her keep going.

2. BUILDING YOUR RESILIENCE

The APA suggests four ways to help build resilience. These are listed below with prompts for reflection.

Purpose: Consider your purpose for writing and connect with your motivation by setting goals and tracking your progress.

Healthy thinking: Use the 'obstacle thinking' approach to acknowl-edge the regular challenges you face, learn from past experiences through reflection, and plan ahead.

Connection: Think about how you can work with other writers, be part of a community, and support people.

Wellness: Productivity is predicated on being able to do the work, so sleep, eat, move, take breaks and gather ideas so you can write.

3. GET MOVING AGAIN WITH SOMETHING SMALL

We all get stuck in different ways, but the outcome is the same: the writing slows, we can't figure out a way forward, writing sessions feel arduous and inaction takes hold. How you get writing again will be personal to you, but one approach to get you moving again is to *start small*.

When you set yourself an overly ambitious writing goal you risk triggering the fear centres in your brain. It's far better to do something little that nudges your writing forward rather than trying and failing to achieve something too big. Getting a few quick wins under your belt is far more productive and positive long term than having large, over-whelming goals that never go anywhere.

Consider your overall goal or project, then scale back. It could be that you write for less time or fewer words. Focus on the process, not the outcome for now.

When you've reached the end of your writing session, zoom in and keep focussed. What will you do next time? Plan ahead, step by step. Take it slow, make it small – it all adds up. Revisit Chapter 5 for the science of small.

4. DO SOMETHING DIFFERENT

It's easy to fall into ruts about how to get the writing done. Just like Harrison Moore countered the myth of 'how to be an academic' by experimenting and being playful, the solution to getting unstuck is doing something different.

- ← If you believe you can only write in long periods of time, try writing in a short chunks of time. Write spontaneously and grab pieces of time when you can.
- ← If you feel certain that you must write thousands of words but you're not making any progress, write less. Set a limit to write a paragraph, 100 words, a sentence.
- ← If typing feels like the only proper way to write, mix up the medium: write by hand – voice record your ideas, create a

presentation with slides, pen a poem. Free yourself to create by using a different format and approach.

↩ If you feel stuck or too tired to write, take the ten-minute test. Set a timer and start writing. When the ten minutes are up, check in with yourself. If you are too tired, stop. You tried and it didn't work, so drop the guilt. If it worked, do another ten minutes. Don't assume – test.

↩ If you believe that the best thing to do right now is to grind it out and stay at your desk – do the opposite. Get up, take a break, go outside. Test the assumption – you never know, a change of scene might shake things up.

5. BE KIND TO YOURSELF

When you feel stuck, this can often turn into frustration. So, as a means to punish yourself further, you decide you won't allow yourself time to clear your head for just one minute.

When you feel like this, the very best thing to do for your productivity, and physical and mental health, is to stop and get perspective. Sticking with it is demotivating, damaging and counterproductive. Writing will always involve moments that make you want to tear your hair out. The answer is to notice when you're feeling like this and know how to respond.

If you're prone to moments of self-flagellation, it can be helpful to write a 'note to self' to remind yourself how best to climb out of a rut. You can pin it up at your desk or create a list of things to do that will reinvigorate you.

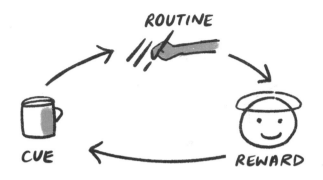

CUE · ROUTINE · REWARD

CHAPTER 8

TRACKING

YAY

WHOOP!

REWARD
CELEBRATE
TREAT

8

HABIT

*Stop wishing for a writing routine –
trigger one and make it stick
with rewards*

It could have been so very different. Author Daniel Pink calls regret a 'uniquely painful and uniquely human emotion' – far more than, say, mere disappointment – because it involves us blaming ourselves for doing, or not doing, certain things in our lives. [1] His survey of nearly 5,000 Americans finds that respondents overwhelmingly regretted things they didn't do compared to those they did by more than three to one. However, he goes on to say that the fact that we experience regret can make us better in the end. Regrets shape our future, and sometimes even the very thought of having one is enough to spur us into action and make radical changes to our lives. That was the case for Wyl Menmuir when he imagined a future where he told his kids that he could have written a novel, and they replied, 'Oh yeah dad... you could have.'

At the time Menmuir was head of English, working as a senior manager in a large school. It should have been his dream job, teaching kids to read and write, but he said, 'I wasn't happy. I needed to be writing – that's all I've wanted to do my whole life.' Like many of us, he lacked the confidence to change. Unlike many of us, his life was upended by tragedy. 'When we lost our son, who was stillborn,

I had the realisation how finite life was. What if I didn't do all of these things that I want to do? If I get further down the line and I've missed the chance to do those things.'

In the midst of his grief, he realised he had to take something positive away from this experience. He stopped making excuses. He quit his safe job for freelance insecurity. Those first few weeks were filled with fear, but learning to live with fear has brought him many adventures, from learning to pothole (spelunking), to free diving, surfing, and sailing from Svalbard through Arctic waters. It also gave him the initial push to get writing.

But Menmuir realised he needed more than just an initial surge of activity – it needed to be sustained. He'd done a few writing courses and got a place on a part-time Masters of Creative Writing course, but he was struggling to build a regular writing routine. That's when we met. It was December 2013 and we were about to launch a trial of a digital writing habits tracker called Write Track. We were looking for testers to sign up for a research project kicking off in January. Menmuir had heard about it on the writing grapevine and emailed us to volunteer.

Write Track was a website that set out to solve the problem Bec had spotted when she worked at the writers' retreat centre. Arvon had been running retreats since 1968, and over the course of half a century the offer had been honed to perfection. Lumb Bank was the ideal writing environment; the time and space to write, with inspiration and support from some of the best writers in their fields. The tutors who ran the courses nurtured, encouraged, and gave one-to-one feedback to the visiting writers. Every meal was catered, every need was met, there was no wifi and the mobile signal was dodgy at best, all of which made Lumb Bank a respite from the demands and distractions of everyday life. Yet, for some writers, the writing decreased or stopped when they returned home.

Environment fosters routine, habits are forged in a context; change the setting and the behaviour is lost.

At the time, Bec was tracking all sorts of health, diet and exercise behaviours on her iPhone. It got her thinking: what if there was a similar tool for writing, something that took the elements used in health trackers and applied it to creative habits like writing? That's the promise of habits, the hypothesis that we set out to test with writers. After more than a year of research, supported by academics working on human-computer interaction, the evidence was clear. Writing habits were hard to develop and yet highly sought: 85 per cent of respondents wanted to write more regularly, and of these a remarkable 90 per cent wanted to write every day.[2] A writing habit was the magic bullet that Menmuir was looking for when he signed up for the trial. He's not alone.

A BRIEF HISTORY OF HABITS

Humans have been debating how to build good habits for millennia. Stoic philosopher Epictetus said: 'Every habit and faculty is maintained and increased by the corresponding actions: the habit of walking by walking, the habit of running by running. If you would be a good reader, read; if a writer, write.'[3] His observation rings true – habits are formed by repeating the desired behaviour. However, for anyone who has tried and failed to walk, run, read or write more, we know that there is more to habits than reason and repetition. We are not creatures of reason; sheer force of will is not enough for us to develop new habits, however much we may want them. That's where psychology picks up from ancient philosophy.

William James, the father of American psychology, observed that all living creatures are 'bundles of habits'.[4] His ground-breaking work *The Principles of Psychology* foreshadows modern neuroscience with its emphasis on plasticity. He investigated how many of our daily tasks run automatically, powered by habits of which we have no conscious knowledge. 'Few people,' he wrote, 'can tell off-hand which sock, shoe or trouser leg they put on first.' When questioned they can't explain what they do, yet their hands never make a mistake. This automatic behaviour is witnessed not just in simple tasks like getting dressed, but in everyone who practises a long-familiar handicraft. Though he doesn't single out writers, they are akin to his musicians, carpenters and knitters. As such, he said: 'Habit is thus the enormous fly-wheel of society.'[5]

In 1903, a decade after *Principles* was published, the *American Journal of Psychology* defined habits as being 'acquired through previous repetition of a mental experience'.[6] Like philosophers hundreds of years prior, these early psychologists noted the repeated nature of an action of habit, and it's instinctively what we think of when we consider habits. In short, a habit is a behaviour which, through repetition, becomes automatic.

They're also behaviours that many of us want to do more or less of. Step forward Professor Wendy Wood, one of the world's foremost experts in how habits are formed. Her research examined the role of rewards in habit formation. She found that 43 per cent of what people do every single day is repeated in the same context, usually while they are thinking about something else. She said that people are 'automatically responding without really making decisions. And that's what a habit is. A habit is a sort of a mental shortcut to repeat what we did in the past that worked for us and got us some reward.'[7]

Habits are performed with little or no conscious thought; they are by definition automatic, more of a reflex than a choice. There have been many studies that measure how long it takes for 'automaticity' to kick in and a habit to stick. Before you ask, there is no milestone number of repetitions to hit – research and hearsay have suggested everything from 21 to 66 days, but the answer depends on what you are trying to do, the driving forces and the context in which you find yourself.

Back to Menmuir and his writing ambitions. He had a strong driving force and had already made some drastic changes like quitting his job and committing to a three-year Masters of Arts programme. He'd been on a handful of writing courses to explore short stories, out of which emerged an idea for a novel. But he didn't yet have a regular writing habit to make it all happen. Luckily, he realised that and took action by volunteering for our research project.

TRACKING FOR SUCCESS

Menmuir signed up to test Write Track, a prototype designed to investigate whether technology can foster and support a writing habit.* Dubbed 'Fitbit for Writing', it asked writers to set a writing goal and track their progress against it. There were several other features, including reminders and nudges to write. 'It massively helped,' said Menmuir, 'in so many different ways, partly in the daily tracking of what I have written today. It sounds like a really simple thing, but all I needed was simple things. Just putting a little comment underneath: *This is how I'm feeling right now.*'

At the end of the study, nearly all (92 per cent) of frequent users like Menmuir felt they had made progress, agreeing that it helped them reflect on their writing, with over three-quarters (77 per cent) saying it helped them improve their productivity. When the test

---

* Presenting at an academic conference, we argued that the Write Track prototype was: 'a focus on positive behaviour change and fostering habits which can be tracked by the individual writer. The suggestion that goal-setting and habit change could be a more effective route to writing success than, for example, generating ideas, was tested with a large group of writers.'

came to a close, Menmuir and some of the other testers carried on using the tracker. That's where things get really interesting.

Menmuir kept on writing and logging his progress against his goals and recording how he felt about it. Over the next two years, he inputted lots of data, from those first few sessions when he was exploring an idea for a novel, to hitting his first 10,000 words, all the way through to finishing a full draft, logging when the novel was picked up by indie press Salt Publishing. In the summer of 2016, *The Many* was published and within days of landing on bookshelves, it was announced that it had made the Booker Prize longlist, one of the world's most prestigious literary prizes. With a mix of quantifiable data such as time, date and word counts alongside personal reflections, Menmuir tracked his writing progress from idea to publication. While the purpose of his tracking was to help himself, it provides a unique insight into how writing habits are built – one we can all learn from.

As a debut writer without any publishing record, getting longlisted for the Booker Prize generated a lot of interest in Menmuir's life and his writing process. The judges of the prize said that *The Many* was 'the first Man Booker longlisted book to be beholden to an internet group'.[8] With the media spotlight on full beam, we handed all his tracking data over to a team of specialists at the *Guardian*, whose analysis was published as a data visualisation.[9] One thing that was striking was how Menmuir's actual writing routine differed from his plan.

There is a concept in psychology called the 'planning fallacy' – the tendency we all have to underestimate the time it will take us to complete something while knowing full well that similar tasks have taken longer in the past. First proposed in 1979 by Daniel Kahneman and Amos Tversky, it's based in an innate biological bias towards optimism. Menmuir set out to write 500 words a day, five days a week. This goal was inspired by Graham Greene, who aimed for this daily word count, even making it a trait for his main character, the writer Maurice Bendrix, in his novel *The End of the Affair*.[10] If Menmuir had written in 'Greenes' and stuck to the plan, he would have completed his first draft in just 124 days. Instead it took him 671 days.

While tracking can feel like the antithesis of the creative process, it's the secret to sidestepping the planning fallacy trap. When you track, you build up data on how long a project is actually taking you – not how long you'd like it to take or think it will take. This gives you a realistic grounding for making better decisions. Professor Yael Grushka-Cockayne, who studies decision-making in business, explains it this way: 'Tracking historical plans and actuals is the fundamental first step in overcoming the planning fallacy. You should track your performance because if you start with that – let alone anything more sophisticated – you will improve.'[11]

Menmuir found that the act of tracking was one of the things that helped him to get to the end of a manuscript. 'I think it's because it's hard to see the progress you are making when you're writing something as long as a novel,' he said.[12] It takes time, commitment and persistence to write a book, a thesis, screenplay, or a collection of articles or short stories. None of these writing projects is a simple goal, and research shows there is world of difference between achieving a goal and changing your behaviour long term.

HOW TO BUILD A WRITING HABIT
Most New Year's resolutions fail – many crash and burn a few days into January, some are hard won but lost after a few months. One study found that over three-quarters of people managed to stick to their pledges for a week, but two years later less than a quarter had continued.[13] Keeping going with a pledge requires long-term

behaviour change, the sort of activity facilitated by habit. When looking at behaviour change, we need to forget notions of self-control and willpower – these might be helpful in the short term, but they are not sufficient to lead to long-term change. Professor Wendy Wood tells us to stop trying so hard: 'Challenge,' she writes, 'is not the point. No pride in forming habits in the teeth of resistance. Remove the friction, set the right driving forces and let the good habits roll into your life.'[14]

Wood explains that there are three bases to effective habit formation: repetition, context and reward. We talked earlier about repetition, in that it's the outward sign of a habit, a behaviour that is repeated without conscious thought. Next, we need to get inside the brain and take a closer look at the neuroscience of habits.

All habits start with a decision to do something – it could be a goal such as writing a book, learning to drive or cooking a new recipe. If you were hooked up to an fMRI scanner the first time you did one of these, the part of the brain associated with planning, self-control and abstract thought would light up. This includes the pre-frontal cortex and mid-brain, known as the 'associative loop'. As you repeat a task, over time it rewires your brain, firing up another neural network known as the 'sensorimotor network'. On the outside the tasks you do are the same, yet on the inside a completely different part of the brain is working, allowing you to respond more automatically and reducing the number of conscious decisions you need to make. You stop having to try so hard. It becomes routine, so that the actions and the order you do them in are 'cued' up. As Wood writes, 'habit is a mental association between a context cue and a response that develops as we repeat an action in that context for a reward'.[15]

This neurological process is often called the 'habit loop'.[16] The reward at the end helps your brain figure out if this particular

The Habit Loop

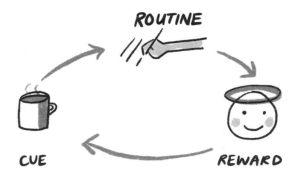

loop is worth remembering for the future. The more the loop is repeated, cycling from the context cue to the reward, the more it becomes ingrained. Eventually it is automatic and the routine becomes a habit.

As Nobel and Pulitzer prize-winning novelist John Steinbeck describes in his journal, if he were given the choice, he wouldn't write at all: 'In writing, habit seems to be a much stronger force than either willpower or inspiration.'[17] The force is found in setting up the right context that cues the writing, rather than prompting another routine. Here's how to trigger some writing and start reaping those rewards.

COFFEE AND CONTEXT: EXPLORING CUES TO WRITE

So, how can a writing habit become embedded in our lives? The first step is to find your trigger. For Menmuir, it's coffee. 'I don't think I can write without it,' he says, and he's certainly not alone. Earlier in the book we heard how Anthony Trollope had his groom bring him coffee at the start of a writing session. Likewise, Patricia Highsmith swore by cigarettes and doughnuts to accompany her coffee, Proust was partial to café au lait, and Gertrude Stein claimed that coffee gave her more time to think.* Menmuir said, 'Coffee will happen at the beginning and then I will have coffee at the end.' For Menmuir and countless other writers, coffee cues up the routine to write. It's a trigger to type – although what gets you going might be very different. After noticing how he bundled coffee with writing, Menmuir became more intentional about it, using an if/when-then plan using a mental shortcut that states: 'If coffee, then Scrivener.'† However, on bad days, he settles down at his desk with a coffee then checks emails or Twitter. While he intended to write, a whole other habit is triggered and the loop isn't leading him to writing but to distraction.

Context is a force on our behaviour and includes everything in the world surrounding us. It's the environment we're in, the location, the people around us, time of day and the actions we have just done.[18] And how close we are to those cues makes a difference, as we'll engage with what is near us and overlook what is further away. We see this in how supermarkets place tempting sweets and chocolate as we're queuing for the checkout, and how the mere presence of a smartphone distracts and leaves us drained.[19] Understanding how context cues up habits can help us foster good routines, like opening Scrivener, and avoid bad habits, like checking Twitter. But don't worry if, like Menmuir, you occasionally slip – the odd lapse doesn't destroy an emerging habit. A study from Wood's lab found that participants embarking on a new routine could miss a day or two without derailing what they'd started.[20]

---

* If you like reading about the routines of writers and creatives, check out Mason Currey's two-book series *Daily Rituals*, where we found some of these examples. They are a treasure trove of writerly quirks.

† Scrivener is a computer programme designed for long-form writing projects and much beloved (obsessively so) by novelists, screenwriters, academics and non-fiction writers.

HOW REWARDS EMBED A HABIT

The final foundation of habit formation is reward. Engaging the reward circuitry of the brain to associate something pleasurable with the behaviour makes it more likely you'll repeat the routine. But the key is timing. For the habit loop to work effectively, the reward must be delivered either during the routine or milliseconds afterwards. In that instant, dopamine is released in the reward centre of the brain, processed, and new neural pathways are formed that will embed the habit. As Wood explains, dopamine sets a timescale to habit learning, spiking immediately with a reward. 'Unanticipated rewards in the future, such as a paycheck bonus in two months or an athletic trophy you get at the end of a season, will not change neural connections in the same way. Rewards have to be experienced right after we do something in order to build habit associations (context-response) in memory.'[21] So, while long-term rewards like publication, prizes and rave reviews might urge us on, they won't embed a habit.

In a previous chapter we met Tiny Habits® master, B.J. Fogg. 'Your brain,' he says, 'has a built-in system for encoding new habits, and by celebrating you can hack the system. When you find a celebration that works for you, and you do it immediately after a new behavior, your brain repatterns to make that behavior more automatic in the future.'[22] It can be hard to find a celebration that works for you. It is, after all, deeply personal and also dependent on your culture. For example, for rather introverted, self-critical, buttoned-up Brits like us, celebration tends to come less easily than to our more exuberant American friends. The key to celebration is for it to feel authentic (you can't fake a celebration because your brain will know you are lying), to do it immediately, and for it to have enough intensity to trigger dopamine.

To build a habit using the reward circuitry of the brain, you need to choose a celebration, start doing it when you complete your routine, and be consistent. However, you don't need to keep doing it. With time the habit loop will become automatic; the habit is established and you can stop celebrating. Or, for our friends in the US, keep whooping, leaping and fist-pumping just for the sheer joy of it. Which brings us to treats.

TREATS, MILESTONES AND STREAKS

The promise of habit is compelling. It removes the effort of deciding why/when/where and how to write and the cognitive load of willpower by triggering a non-conscious routine that makes the writing automatic. Habits are often touted as the magic solution to our struggles: they can transform our lives, help us achieve our most ambitious goals and fulfil long-held dreams. They are full of promise – habits are learned; our behaviour can change, we can stop bad habits (procrastinating with Twitter) and build good habits (such as writing 500 words every day).

Yet, many writers unwittingly fall into the *if only I had a writing habit* trap and then blame themselves when they fail. We see this all the time with the writers we work with. They do the groundwork that sets them on the path to change, they decide to write, have an idea, an intention, a goal, a plan and know exactly what step to take first. Yet, writing never comes easily, it's never automatic.

This got us thinking whether writing can ever be truly habitual. It's hard, it takes time and effort – you have to be organised, motivated and determined. The rewards in writing are distant, many months or years away. Writing doesn't give you the dopamine high of instant gratification in the way that, say, gambling or online gaming does. Many writers find writing painful, and yet something is driving them to continue.

What our adventures into writing habits taught us is that one of the keys to successful behaviour change – the kind of effort required when working on long-term goals like writing – is to make it more pleasurable. While this is heresy in habit circles, incentives can play a part. The definition of an incentive is 'something that incites or tends to incite to action or greater effort, as a reward offered for increased productivity'.[23] In other words, a treat. We like to think of them as closer to a bribe that gives you something to look forward to, a reward for your effort, a pleasure to associate with writing. That's the function of Menmuir's coffee at the end of a writing session. While it is thoroughly enjoyable, it is not a habit-inducing, neural-pathway-creating, brain-boosting reward. That's because there is too large a gap between the routine of writing and the drinking of coffee to trigger dopamine and create a neural link between the two. The coffee in this case is a treat, which acts as an incentive, not as a reward. While his coffee might not meet the standards of an immediate neural-firing reward, it can help him to keep writing.

Happiness and habits author Gretchen Rubin said: 'Treats may sound like a self-indulgent, frivolous strategy, but it's not. Because forming good habits can be draining, treats can play an important role. When we give ourselves treats, we feel energized, cared for, and contented, which boosts our self-command – and self-command helps us maintain our healthy habits.'[24] Without treats, we begin to feel burned-out, depleted, and resentful of the writing, the one thing we want to do above all else!

As well as treating yourself after the writing, we encourage writers to identify 'good things' every time they write. This is a type of cognitive restructuring that helps associate positive feelings with your work-in-progress rather than the default negative ones. Bestselling novelist Meg Mason used a similar approach to get out of her bad writing attitude; some days the only good thing she found was the font.[25] Professor Martin Seligman, the founder of positive psychology, found that noticing good things and expressing gratitude for them can have a long-term impact on wellbeing. In one study he asked participants to identify and write down three good things each day – the positive effects of this were felt for six months. Not only will it help you associate positive feeling with your writing, but the effects could also spread to other areas of your life.

The final way to bring pleasure into the slog of writing is by celebrating milestones. The data experts from the *Guardian* spotted that Menmuir always celebrated milestones around the 10,000-word mark. It took him three months to reach the first milestone and another nine months to hit 20,000. He tracked at the time: 'Over 10,000 words in now, so this feels like the first tangible step on the road to achieving my write-a-novel dream.' Menmuir has continued to mark his milestones, explaining: 'I learned from that first experience of treating myself every 10,000 words. I will go for a surf or a long run, or I'll go for a beer and read a book in a pub for an hour, just to say you've achieved something. Marking those milestones is another way of making sure I continue – of making sure that I finish – and that's the key thing.'

While marking milestones is a great way to incentivise over the long haul, don't forget that habit is the culmination of small actions repeated regularly. That's why Menmuir continues to track his progress. He explains that years after the Write Track experiment ended and the digital tracker was closed down, he still tracks the number of words he writes and the days he writes, logging the number of unbroken days he's worked. 'It might seem a bit childish,' he says, 'but when I see the row of crosses in the diary or stars on the screen – then it encourages me to continue.'

Jerry Seinfeld famously marked a calendar with a cross for every day that he wrote. 'After a few days you'll have a chain. Just keep at it and the chain will grow longer every day. You'll like seeing that chain, especially when you get a few weeks under your belt. Your only job is to not break the chain.'[26] Once you've got a streak going, you don't want to break it. There's intrinsic pleasure to be had from seeing progress, a hit of dopamine that rewards each cross, more so when the chain grows. When you commit to building a streak it becomes part of your identity – if you take a day off it feels weird, which encourages you to pick up the streak the next day.

If you've read this book chapter by chapter, you'll have identified what you want to write, figured out how to fit writing into your life and have a first step to get started. Planning will get you started, but if every writing session involved that cognitive load you'd end up drained and depleted. The promise of a habit spares you that effort. By understanding how habits are formed, you can trigger your writing, develop a routine and embed the habit with rewards that will keep you going day after day. The exercises that follow will show you how.

The Writer's Sandbox – Habit

1. IDENTIFY THE ROUTINE

John Updike said: 'A solid routine saves you from giving up.' The routine in habit terms is the behaviour you want to develop. Take time to consider what a writing routine might look like. When do you want to write, where, and what will you do when you show up each day? Imagine it fully – visualise, draw, brainstorm, explore and make notes on what a successful routine looks like for you.

2. IDENTIFY THE CONTEXT

The context is the cue that sets up the routine in the habit loop. It's a trigger to action, prompting behaviours you want to do. Charles Duhigg found that most cues fit into one of five categories:[27]

1. **Location** – where you write. Brainstorm all the environments you can write in. You want to avoid triggering another habit – for example, if you write at the kitchen table you may catch yourself washing up, or at your work desk you may end up managing your inbox. Can you design your environment or create a ritual to trigger writing, such as setting up cues like putting out your notebook?
2. **Time** – when you write. Is there a good time of day for writing? Consider if you are an early bird or a night owl. Tap into your natural chronotype[28] to make the most of your energy and attention. Or consider if there's a time of day you are less likely to get distracted.
3. **Emotional state** – how you feel affects your behaviour. Take a cue from your emotional state to write. Use feelings to fuel your writing – if you're frustrated with work, grab your notepad rather than send an angry email to your boss. If you're feeling great, then free write and generate ideas.

4. **Other people** can help you write. Can you find other writers to buddy up with? What about finding supporters to share your projects with? Think of readers, mentors and creativity cheerleaders. Enlist others to trigger your writing, to learn from and also make it more fun. There's more ideas on this in the next chapter.

5. **Immediately preceding** – use existing behaviours to attach writing to. Think about your day and what you could do before writing. For example, doing morning pages as soon as you wake up, writing after you've eaten lunch, or when you sit on your train home. As a bonus, use a visual trigger to set it up – for example, keep a notepad on your bedside table to trigger morning writing or set a notification for writing time in your calendar.

3. FIND A REWARD BY EXPERIMENTING

The reward embeds a routine by triggering dopamine and associating pleasure with the behaviour. B.J. Fogg said: 'People change best by feeling good, not by feeling bad.' His research found that the people who embraced celebration were the most successful in creating habits quickly.[29]

There's no such thing as a universal reward – one person's treat is another's trick – so think about what will motivate you. Start by imagining a scenario where you might spontaneously celebrate. What would you do when you watch your sports team win? When you get an amazing job offer? When you type the words 'The End' as you complete a long writing project? Imagine your reaction and use that.

Keep experimenting with your routines and rewards. Anne Rice said, 'I certainly have a routine, but the most important thing, when I look back over my career, has been the ability to change routines.'[30] So change it up. Experiment to develop new, better, more fulfilling writing habits. Likewise, getting the same reward is boring to our brains. We crave novelty, which is why gambling is so addictive. Think of ways you can challenge yourself and reap variable rewards.

4. BRIBE YOURSELF

If you're struggling to design the perfect dopamine-kick for your habit, relax. Step back and look at your writing routine and find ways to make it more pleasurable. Think of treats or incentives rather than immediate rewards. Start by considering what will generate positive feelings as you write. If you need an incentive to bribe good behaviour – what does that look like?

One trick is to use your common procrastination activities as rewards rather than delaying tactics. In short – *Twitter after writing, not before!*

5. REWARD THE EFFORT, NOT THE OUTCOME

The amount of effort you put into writing can't always be measured by word count. Sometimes writing in short energetic bursts can move your work on in leaps and bounds. Other days you spend hours and barely produce a workable sentence. So, reward the effort you put in, not the outcome. This is particularly important if you are celebrating milestones. If your reward is too small, then you'll lose motivation with your project. However, if your reward is too big then it all becomes about getting the prize rather than what you need to do to get there.

6. HAVE A PLAN

It can take a while to embed a writing routine, and once you have one, it can be disrupted or lost. Rather than rely on willpower, you need a plan. This can be as simple as noting it down, for example – *I will write every weekday at 8am for one hour at the café opposite the train station.*

This example is clear and specific; it uses an everyday activity like commuting to attach the new writing behaviour to. It gives a place, time and regularity so it's clear when it's been achieved, and has the bonus of building in a reward with hot coffee and cakes.

Another approach to planning is to use the if/when-then format. Create a sentence like Wyl Menmuir did: 'That's where I've become a better writer, when I use "if this, then that". "If coffee, then Scrivener" is a really useful trigger to write.'

7. ASSOCIATE GOOD THINGS WITH WRITING

Get in the habit of noticing good things about your writing. It will help you seek out, notice and appreciate good things as they happen, it will make you feel more positive about your writing and will power you for the long haul.

8. DON'T BREAK THE CHAIN

Track your progress like Jerry Seinfeld – start a writing streak and see how long it lasts. Another idea is to sign up to a challenge such as 100 Days of Writing (see Jenn Ashworth, Chapter 2). Just search for the #100daysofwriting hashtag on Instagram or Twitter and find a community of writers. Austin Kleon says: 'Practice every day. Put an X in the box. After 100 Days, you will suck less.'[31]

9. BELIEVE YOU CAN DO IT

Writers have a tricky relationship with self-belief. Whether you're starting out, have a publication pipeline or a solid backlist, there's always an opportunity for your inner critic to eat away at your confidence. Having the support of others can give you a much-needed boost – as we'll talk about in the next chapter. Join a community of writers to find a group of like-minded people with the same goal as you. If you're feeling shy, start small. Researchers found that having just one other person is enough to make you believe change is possible – so find a writing buddy.

10. DON'T DESPAIR

Professor Wendy Wood found that if you do fall off the wagon, you needn't despair or give up hope – the habit is not lost. Acknowledge you have slipped and use it as an opportunity to make your context stronger and clearer. Revisit the cues above and try again. Remember the advice from Daniel Pink and use the momentary regret of not writing to spur you on.

Our habits guide helps you identify the cues and rewards you need to make writing more routine. To download it, go to: **prolifiko.com/ writtenresources**

COMPETE or COLLABORATE

CHAPTER 9

ACCOUNTABILITY

9

PEOPLE

Figure out your people preferences to harness the power of accountability

Academic authors have been the subject of more studies looking at writing productivity and process than any other group. This is partly because researchers often look no further than their own university backyards for guinea pigs, and partly because that's where the pressure to write is often most acute. We mentioned earlier a phrase that's well known in scholarly circles: 'Publish or perish.' When academics don't write and publish regularly, their careers can nosedive – and so do their institution's bank balances and reputation.

As a result, universities and colleges across the world have tried all sorts of initiatives – workshops, retreats, mentoring schemes, coaching programmes, you name it – to cajole and support time-poor professors and struggling students to keep the writing flowing. And academics being academics, there have been countless papers written about the pros and cons of these initiatives. One review of seventeen separate studies looked at the effectiveness of three types of intervention: writing groups, one-to-one support and writing courses.[1] It concluded that all three methods can certainly improve publication rates, writing quality and skill to an extent, but that writing support groups of one kind or another perform particularly well in terms of improving what the researchers call the 'psycho-social benefits'.*

What they mean by this is that there's something about these writing groups – whether it's the feel-good factor and camaraderie they create, or the support and accountability they provide – that is exceptionally good at helping people to keep going. And not only that, mutual support groups like these can cause what the researchers call a 'ripple effect' throughout an entire university campus. New researchers feel inspired to write. Stuck writers feel more motivated. Those who had put their writing on hold prioritise it again. When universities set up and encourage writing groups, this breeds a culture of support that improves productivity, confidence and motivation more widely.

You might not need them or us to tell you that joining a writing group of one kind or another can perk up your writing productivity. You may have tried this method yourself. It's certainly a piece of advice we give out often when we see writers slogging it out alone. We've seen time and time again how writing alongside other people gives people confidence and provides encouragement to keep going through the rough patches. Habits expert Charles Duhigg explains that other people can even make it easier for us to get into a writing routine because change is easier, more possible and more likely in the company of others. 'Belief is easier when it occurs within a community,' he writes.[2] Quite simply, other people enable you to accomplish things you'd struggle to do solo.

So, you might ask, if writing groups are such a universal good, why waste any more ink on the topic? But not so fast. While our own experience and the research suggests writing groups,

---

* For more, see Rowena Murray's *Writing in Social Spaces: A Social Processes Approach to Academic Writing*.

communities and collaborations can bring huge benefits, there are factors you should consider before you dive in. How you engage with them and what format you should choose depends entirely on you – and that's what this chapter is all about.

To get going and explain this point further, let's delve into the blood-soaked and whiskey-fuelled history of the world's most pre-eminent and successful creative writing programme.

BULLIES AND BULLWHIPS

The fact Paul Engle, the director of the Iowa Writers' Workshop (IWW) from 1941 to 1965, wrote with a bullwhip next to his typewriter speaks volumes about his methods and the philosophy behind the original programme. Based at the University of Iowa, the workshop has produced an astonishing number of distinguished writers and poets since its establishment in 1936. John Irving, Ann Patchett, Raymond Carver, Richard Ford, Kurt Vonnegut – its alumni list is a rollcall of the greatest American writers of the 20th century. But in the early days, the IWW wasn't for the faint-hearted.

Channelling Charles Darwin, Engle deliberately designed an ego-fuelled, survival-of-the-fittest vibe, where writers' work and self-confidence was regularly crushed by harsh criticism. In the early days, students were often ex-World War Two GIs returning from the front line who all thought they were the next Ernest Hemingway. They would solve their literary disputes in very un-literary ways by having drunken, bloody bar brawls and on-campus boxing matches – often with their tutors. Engle's merciless approach was about driving the writers hard to do one thing and one thing only: write and publish. Refusing to 'coddle the egos of young romantic visionaries', as he put it, Engle deliberately designed the IWW to harden students to the harsh commercial world they'd face on the outside.[3]

He engineered a competitive environment where students would come into direct conflict with each other and jockey for position. He wanted students to feel an intense pressure to publish because he believed that was how you got results. And in many ways, he was right. The workshop's graduates have published far more than any other Master of Fine Arts programme in the world. To date, IWW alumni have written over 3,000 books and won 29 Pulitzer Prizes. The programme has produced six American poet laureates and numerous National Book Award winners. But at what cost? Engle's brutal approach to creative development suited some. But it left very deep scars for others.

American author Flannery O'Connor flourished in Engle's sink-or-swim environment, saying in later life, 'everywhere I go I'm asked if the universities stifle writers. My opinion is that they don't stifle enough of them.'[4] Others, like former poet laureate Rita Dove, felt creatively crushed. A student of the IWW in the 1970s, Dove left with her confidence in tatters. She felt hemmed in by rigid rules and structures and was so traumatised at one point that she stopped writing for a year. Novelist Sandra Cisneros had a similarly disastrous experience. Her time at the workshop was so bad that she quit to set up an alternative programme, the Macondo Writers Workshop. 'Macondo is a workshop that gathers writers who are generous, compassionate, and believe their writing can make non-violent social change,' she explained. 'In other words, the opposite of the Iowa Writers' Workshop.'[5] Her writing programme was more gentle, supportive and collaborative in its approach, something that can be just as powerful as a dog-eat-dog environment.*

---

* Such an environment is no place for the vulnerable. In 1951, Robert Shelley, an IWW student and poet, took his own life.

COMPETE OR COLLABORATE?

In 2016 a team of behaviour-change specialists decided to examine what social conditions best motivated people to maintain an active lifestyle (desk-bound writers take note).[6] We're sharing it with you to demonstrate how important it is that you choose a group environment that's right for you. The researchers told three groups of sedentary office workers that they had to try to improve their fitness over the course of four weeks. But the ways they were going to do this would be different.

> **Group 1** were the collaborators. They were given a group target they had to reach together.

> **Group 2** were the competitors. They were told to compete against each other for prizes and their progress would be displayed for all to see on a leader board.

> **Group 3** were the control. They were given a few public health leaflets to read about the benefits of activity.

Now, you may not be too surprised to learn that the control group never really left their swivel chairs. By comparison, the collaborators were far more active, improving their activity levels by 16 per cent over the month – a good result. But it was the competitors who experienced the largest improvements. They increased their activity levels by nearly a third (30 per cent). So, the case for competing seems clear.

Before you start googling 'bullwhips for sale', the results need closer inspection. The data shows that the collective activity levels of the competitors and collaborators were similar until the final week. But then, something surprising happened. In the last week, two people made super-human leaps in their activity levels and so skewed the overall figure for the competitor group. 'This reflects the fact that in competitive environments those who are doing better than the average are likely to feel motivated and continue their improvement, whereas those who find themselves below the average can feel demoralised and give up,' the researchers conclude. Or in other words, competing created two participants who swam fast while the rest sank, while collaborating lifted the performance of the whole group but created no superstars.

What this teaches us is the importance of finding an environment that suits you and your personality. Competitive or collaborative environments aren't inherently 'bad' or 'good'. If you're a competitive sort, collaborative environments may bore you. If you thrive with more support, competitive conditions may damage your progress. Writing groups are the same. Would you thrive in Engle's tough-love environment? Or instead, would you prefer a more nurturing environment offered by a group like the Macondo Writers Workshop? Because if you would, we're now going to explore why a non-competitive environment can work just as well.

THE POWER OF BELONGING

It's 2003 and the dot-com bubble has burst. At the centre is San Francisco, where Rennie Saunders is creative director of one of the city's once-buzzing agencies. But now, his company is suffering. It's losing staff, technology clients, and things are looking bad. But instead of digging in further, hoping it will all blow over or living in fear of his career, Saunders decides to turn the crisis into an opportunity. He quits the lucrative tech scene to pursue his long-held ambition of becoming an author – a dream he's had since the age of ten.

But soon after quitting, Saunders encounters a problem. He begins to miss the structure of his job. Although he has ample time to write, things start to get in the way – procrastination takes hold. At work, he had colleagues he felt accountable to and a boss setting him targets and giving him deadlines. But now, it's just him, alone in a room with his writing. He is finding it harder and harder to show up with nobody else to answer to – so he comes up with a novel approach. Rather than attending more writer meetups (which were useful but all too easy to avoid), he starts to organise them instead. And this gives him the impetus he needs to show up. 'When the meetup's in the calendar and you have people coming along, you show up yourself. You don't want to let people down,' he told us. 'In a funny way I guess I tricked myself to getting the writing done.'

Trickery or not, it was an approach that worked. Within eighteen months of organising the first writer meetup at San Francisco's Crossroads Café in August 2007, Saunders wrote three novels, countless novellas and a collection of short stories. He went on to run that meetup for the next ten years. He could have stopped there, but he didn't. The popularity of Saunders' sessions ballooned. To meet demand, he organised more of them across San Francisco, recruited volunteers, branched out into other US cities and then to other countries. Today, Rennie Saunders is CEO and founder of global writing phenomenon Shut Up & Write! – and it all started as a way to get himself to sit down and write. When we talk to him in his home office, he's fizzing with excitement because we've asked him his favourite question – what's Shut Up & Write!'s secret sauce?

With a worldwide community of close to 100,000 writers and chapters in hundreds of cities across the world, Saunders says the success of Shut Up & Write! comes down to its simplicity. Unlike Engle's 'survival of the fittest' model at the Iowa Writers' Workshop, Saunders designed his meetups to have absolutely no competitive element whatsoever. This is the secret to their success. Writers write anything. They simply turn up to a café at an appointed time and date – many are complete strangers. The rule is that they write (and do nothing else) for an hour. There is no critiquing, no judgement and no reading aloud afterwards. All the writers are encouraged to do is to tell their fellow Shut Up & Write!-ers how their session went at the end so everyone can learn.

'Writing can be a lonely business. Publishing can be a ruthlessly competitive one,' says James McConnachie from The Society of Authors, 'but authorship is different: it is a fellowship and a community.'[7] At a Shut Up & Write! meetup there is only support and community. Saunders describes the sessions as being like 'safe bubbles'. Normally in a café, people are all doing all sorts of different things – coding (well, it is Silicon Valley), chatting, working or messaging. But in a Shut Up & Write! meetup all of a sudden everyone's doing one thing: writing. 'Everyone puts their creative cap on and it almost becomes a group meditation,' says Saunders. 'People feel safe and by not reading back we're taking away fear and self-judgement.'

● ● ●

Have you ever been in a place like a church, a library or even a sports event or a night club where you're surrounded by complete strangers but feel a connection to them all in some small way? You might have changed your behaviour as a result – been more quiet or more rowdy perhaps? If so, you're experiencing what Stanford University psychologists have dubbed 'mere belonging'. This is a phenomenon which explains that all human beings feel a sense of belonging when they're in a group gathered for a specific reason. Researchers say it has its roots in our evolutionary wiring. Because we feel this sense of belonging, we also feel a sense of accountability and a reluctance to break the social norms of the group. Studies show that merely belonging to a group of people with a loose social connection, like a Shut Up & Write! meetup, with a shared aim or objective makes us more persistent and better able to achieve our goals. 'A mere sense of social connectedness, even with unfamiliar others,' can cause significant changes in the self, personal interests and motivation,' conclude the academics behind the 'mere belonging' idea.[8] Writing in a group with a joint goal in mind makes us more likely to meet that goal than if we wrote on our own.

Saunders says that something magical happens when a group of people – some strangers, some not – meet with the collective aim of writing. It's this 'magic' that author Annie Murphy Paul writes about too as she tries to redefine 'thinking' as something that doesn't just happen inside our heads, but rather as something that happens when we interact with the world. Writing together can give us the extrinsic motivation we need to persist (because letting someone else down is often harder than letting yourself down), but it also gives us something deeper. Murphy Paul writes: 'Group membership acts as a form of *intrinsic* motivation: that is, our behaviour becomes driven by factors internal to the task, such as the satisfaction we get from contributing to a collective effort.'[9] Collaborating with others – even just alongside other people in a shared physical or virtual space – can make the whole process of writing more meaningful, fulfilling and enjoyable. Which in turn gives us the positive associations we need to feel motivated and keep us going. Of course, we can get breakthroughs and 'aha' moments when we write solo – but there's something special when those moments happen together. Perhaps almost invisibly, writing alongside other people makes us more resilient when we're faced with blocks and feel more supported when we're faced with barriers.

● ● ●

So far, we've looked at two ways that working with other people can keep you accountable in groups: through competition or collaboration. But people can work together in a whole host of different ways. Here are a few examples of how writers work in groups, teams or just in pairs to get the writing done. As you read them, think about whether they would work for you.

He burned, she fanned

Writing about the death of his mother Jane, Nick Cornwell describes how at one point the family was searching for photos of her for the order of service at her cremation and found very few.[10] The small number they found were taken before she learned her 'invisibility trick', as Cornwell calls it. She stepped out of photos – even family ones – and declined interviews.

Unbeknownst to all but a few close friends and family, Jane Cornwell played a pivotal role in shaping her husband's writing. While he was 'the writer', they both created the books. Jane edited, revised and shaped the novels behind closed doors. 'All along, at every step, was Jane,' writes her son. 'She was never dramatic; she was ubiquitous and persisting throughout the body of work. He produced, they edited; he burned, she fanned. It was their conspiracy, the thing that no one else could ever offer him, in which they both connived.' Jane and David Cornwell had a relationship that overlapped so far that they created a third identity: John le Carré.

On the same wavelength

While Betty Comden and Adolph Green weren't married, their writing collaboration was so close that plenty of people thought they were. Writing partners for more than 60 years, Comden and Green wrote the scripts and the lyrics to many of Broadway's most iconic musicals like *Singin' in the Rain* – often thought of as the greatest movie musical of all time – and *On the Town*, a musical with a score by Leonard Bernstein starring Frank Sinatra. They also wrote the lyrics for the song everyone thinks they can sing – *New York, New York*.

Being interviewed from Comden's New York apartment where she and Green would work, the couple were asked about their writing process and how they collaborated.[11] They said they were 'interchangeable' in terms of how they worked and said they found it hard to pick apart who had written what, who was better at doing what and whether they had any defined roles at all. 'It's really quite even,' said Comden. 'We often say that at the end of the day we don't know who contributed what idea or what line. We are on the same wavelength and it is sort of instant radar, working out things between us. We find it very easy to work together.'

Only team players allowed

Scriptwriter David Quantick says that working in the writing room on hit sitcom *Veep* is like 'working in a grenade factory where there's no conveyor belt and you have to catch the grenades as they come at you'. Head grenade lobber is Armando Iannucci, who looks for a specific type of person to work in his writing teams. 'To be a good team writer, you have to be a team player,' Iannucci told us. 'So, no ego. You have to be non-proprietorial about your writing.'

Being a member of his writing team involves quickly drafting scripts and jokes and then passing those scripts around to other writers to redraft – the result is a collective effort. Iannucci explains: 'Each writer will have an episode to take charge of, I'll bat back and forward with that writer on the storyline, and ask them to go away and produce a script very quickly,' he said. 'Quick is important because, by the time we come to shoot the episode, almost everything in that script will have changed or been rewritten. So, there's no point being emotionally attached to your dialogue.' While the fast pace of a writing room doesn't suit everyone, one of the benefits of this format is speed – and they can be hugely productive environments. There's simply no time to get blocked.

You can't drop the ball

While writing rooms are common in TV and film, they're rare in other writing fields. However, the author breaking the mould is 'Alice Campion' – who is in fact several authors writing novels together under the same pen name.* The authors first met at a book club in Sydney called the Book Sluts (motto: 'We'll read anything'). They came up with the idea of co-writing a novel on a weekend away discussing Russian literature. The idea – light-hearted at the time – was to write a bestseller to fund a future trip. But what started out as a bit of a laugh to write a Mills & Boon-esque bodice-ripper became more serious as they realised they had stumbled across a good idea for a novel and a highly productive way of writing.

The Alices' writing process evolved as they wrote their first novel. The authors have twice-weekly meetings where the overall story arc and scenes are decided upon. Each author then takes a scene home, agrees a deadline and once done, emails their scene to the group. At the next meeting they read out their scene to the group, mark up feedback and changes, and go home with a different scene to re-write – so each scene is written and then re-written by

---

* The four authors who currently write as Alice Campion are: Jenny Crocker, Jane Richards, Jane St Vincent Welch and Denise Tart. Their first published novel was also co-written with Madeline Oliver.

a different member of the group. This process helped them write their second novel, *The Shifting Light*, in under twelve months – all while having full-time jobs. 'All writers or would-be writers know that the hardest part of the process is to actually write. It's here that group writing can have great advantages. We often liken writing in a group to being in a sporting team – you can't drop the ball when it's your turn to deliver because the whole team will be let down – this definitely helps with procrastination,' they say.

● ● ●

Examples of writing relationships like these prove that other people help and support us to keep motivated in numerous ways. Sometimes writing collaborations can become so close and intertwined that the question of who has written what becomes blurred. This was very much the case with the book you are reading now. However, while this book has been a joint effort, the way we've written it and how we've kept motivated over the months has been very different. We're going to explore this a little more now, but to do so, just like an actor breaking the fourth wall, I'm going to talk directly to you as myself, Chris, for the rest of this chapter.

HOW WE WRITE

If I may, I'd like to paint you a picture of our office – where Bec and I wrote the book you're reading at the moment.* We write from

---

* You might be interested to know that we wrote this book in a similar way to how the Alices wrote their novels. We allocated ourselves different chapters to write, agreed deadlines and then submitted the chapters for review and feedback by the other. After feedback from our editors and beta readers we gave each other different chapters to re-write to ensure that the 'voice' was consistent. We hope we've managed this!

the attic of our house. It's a large-ish square room with an apex roof and Velux windows that let in a little too much sun in the summer and not enough in the winter. The house was built around 1890, so five sturdy oak beams which I've bumped my head on all too frequently span the white-painted sloping ceiling. At the gable end of the room there's an exposed brick arch where the chimney stacks join. It's the kind of thing an estate agent would call a 'feature'. My desk (red glass with oak legs if you were wondering) borders one side of the arch and I sit facing out to the front of the house, while Bec's desk (birch plywood with a blue lino top) is behind me and she sits facing the other way. To my left is a big Yucca plant I've had since university and beyond that, a brown sofa that our Labradoodle, Peggy, lies on if her elderly hips allow her to make it up the stairs (today's a good day). Also, she will normally be snoring. The volume of which has increased as her whiskery beard has greyed over the years.

Neither of us is keen on noise when we write (the snoring is *just* about tolerable). I've never been the kind of person who works with music on in the background. We both drink a lot of tea and take several breaks throughout the day. We find daily exercise is great for concentration. Me: walking, running, gym, squash and tennis. Bec: walking, yoga, gym and, most recently, Zumba. But that's about where our writing similarities end.

You see, we have very different working styles. Over the last year or so that it took us to write the first and second drafts of this book, Bec told her family and friends about her writing – how much she was writing and how far along she was. She signed up to a #100daysofwriting challenge on Instagram and shared her writing progress with others in the community. She committed to writing times by joining online writing groups with the London Writers' Salon and also booked sessions with Focusmate. She's been on writing dates with friends and booked a four-day writing retreat at a residential library. She joined a critiquing group where she shared her work-in-progress for feedback. She's booked writing classes where she learnt aspects of craft. She's paid for a structural edit of this book with particular focus on storytelling and got editorial support as we rewrote. She enlisted the support of beta readers to read the revised draft. She applied for and won a grant that supported her development and paid for her writing time. All of that along with setting writing goals, keeping a writing tracker and reflection diary, and always finding at least one good thing about her writing every day she wrote.

And what tactics did I use to keep going over that same period of time? Nothing. Nada. Zero. I sat at my desk, head down and wrote. Every time I heard the pings of Zoom indicating that Bec was about to start another call, I made a swift exit to the kitchen table where I'd sit and write in silence. Every time she went out to meet a friend to talk about their progress, I stayed in. I have never discussed my writing over coffee, never told anyone about my writing goals, never written with anyone, never shared my progress, most of my friends don't even know I'm co-writing a book (surprise!), and the idea of joining a writing group or community makes me recoil.

I know what you're thinking. You probably think I sound rather curmudgeonly – yes? Perhaps a little, I confess, but I socialise and love to see people. It's just that I've never felt the need for external accountability to get the writing done. Telling other people about my writing doesn't help me in the same way that it helps Bec. I've written all my adult life – as a copywriter, ghost writer and scriptwriter – and I've hit every deadline I've ever been set. Please don't think I'm telling you this to show off. My process isn't 'better' or 'worse' than Bec's (she's also great at hitting all her deadlines). Both have benefits and drawbacks. I'm prone to going it alone too much which means I get stuck in the weeds, while Bec could do with fewer distractions. But in terms of productivity – we both get the work done. So how are we different?*

WHAT ACCOUNTABILITY TYPE ARE YOU?

When Bec and I cover this topic in our coaching and workshops, to help people figure out what kind of accountability structure would work for them, we start with a question. It's a question that divides people into clear groups and certainly gets them talking. I'm going to ask you to consider it now.

Think back to a time when you've wanted to start something new or really stick at something. Think broadly and consider different aspects of your life – for example, starting a fitness regime, learning a new language or musical instrument. Perhaps you've tried to stop doing something, like quitting smoking or giving up meat or sugar. Now, let me ask you this: did you find it easy to stick with that regime entirely on your own or did you need other people urging you on and keeping you accountable? Don't worry, there's no right or wrong answer. I'm asking you these questions because the more you know about yourself, the better equipped you'll be to find an accountability system that works.

You see, we're all motivated differently. Some of us are motivated more by external expectations – the kind other people place on ourselves – while others are more motivated by internal

---

* Several of the early readers of this book scribbled 'gender' (normally in quite big letters) in the margin at this point. Our observation based on coaching writers and working with most of the UK's creative writing course providers and agencies over the last decade is that women tend to seek support more often than men. Research shows this is down to gender norms and societal pressure. The point we're making now is to notice if you do or don't display this tendency and use it to your advantage (ideally to overthrow the patriarchy for the benefit of all genders).

expectations – the kind that we place on ourselves. If you struggle to follow through with a new regime on your own, it's more likely that you're motivated by external expectations and you really hate to let other people down. If you find it easy to stick with new routines and regimes on your own, it's likely that you're more motivated by internal expectations. This means you probably hate letting yourself down. Clearly, not everyone fits neatly into these two camps. You might be somewhere in the middle or you might respond to both in varying degrees.

The writer who developed this concept is Gretchen Rubin, and her work has been pivotal in helping us to support writers find the accountability structures that work for them and their personalities. She developed the Four Tendencies model to categorise how we respond to the expectations placed upon us in four ways.

The Four Tendencies

UPHOLDER

Meets outer expectations
Meets inner expectations

QUESTIONER

Resists outer expectations
Meets inner expectations

OBLIGER

Meets outer expectations
Resists inner expectations

REBEL

Resists outer expectations
Resists inner expectations

In her book she's at pains to make clear that whatever tendency you have isn't 'better' or 'worse' than any other. She writes: 'The happiest, healthiest and most productive people aren't those from a particular Tendency, but rather they're the people who have figured out how to harness the strengths of their Tendency, counteract the weaknesses, and build the lives that work for them.'[12]

Rubin's work made me realise that I'm someone who mainly responds to internal expectation. I've never, for example, had much of a problem with meeting deadlines but I need to know why first. In fact, if I get any kind of request, I'll struggle to do it if I don't understand my 'why'. It's also made me realise that in the past I've probably been a pain to work with (although Bec assures me I've been the perfect co-author of this book and if I had a winking emoji face to insert I'd insert one here), because I feel I have to question every instruction or request ever made of me and won't budge until things make sense to me.

Bec on the other hand, is more motivated by the external expectations placed on her. But she knows this and uses it to her advantage. She really hates letting other people down (she also hates letting herself down too, which means she often gets burned out) and because of this finds workshops, writing groups and account-ability partnerships of one type or another to be vital in helping her to keep writing.

So, what accountability type are you? Are you like me and mainly need to satisfy your own personal expectations, or more like Bec and are more motivated by the expectations other people place on you?* This is important to consider because once you know this,

---

* We heartily recommend that you join the 3 million or so people who have taken Rubin's Four Tendencies Quiz[13] and read her excellent book for a further exposi-tion. And if you were wondering, Chris is a Questioner while Bec's an Upholder.

you can start designing an accountability structure that fits with your personality and your life.

People who are strongly influenced by the expectations others put on them usually put everyone else's needs above their own. Those of us who are strongly influenced by internal expectations can be overly self-critical, which can be just as damaging. However, now you are armed with the knowledge about what your accountability type is, you can take action when you feel stuck or in need of a boost. There are more ideas on how to do this in the exercises at the end of this chapter.

PEOPLE NEED PEOPLE (EVEN INTROVERTS)

While there's no doubt that people need people in different ways and to varying degrees, writing is never a solitary endeavour. While a myth still pervades that true writing and creative geniuses go it alone, a quick flick to the acknowledgements pages of any book will prove this isn't true. No creative project is ever the result of just one mind – even if there's just one name on the cover. I might not need other people to spur me on; but I need the help of other people to bounce ideas off and give me direction. This book is a collaboration after all – the work of two people.

I've always loved this observation from writing scholar and educationalist Helen Sword. She says: 'When we write *for others*, we engage in conversation with our readers. When we write *with others*, we write with colleagues toward a common project. And when we write *among others*, we create a community of writers.'[14] And in these three ways it seems to me that our writing is shaped, encouraged and supported. Even the most private, quiet and introverted writers need others – and to prove that I'll leave you with a short story about one of my personal writing heroes.

According to her biographer, the much-loved writer and enter-tainer Victoria Wood came to regard the youth theatre she joined aged fifteen as her 'salvation' – the first time she felt comfortable about doing anything. Painfully shy, Wood grew up in a remote bungalow in the hills above Bury, Lancashire, in northern England. The youngest of four, she was left to amuse herself as a child: 'I was brought up in one room with a television, a piano and a sandwich,' she later recalled.[15] With few friends, and little contact with her parents and older siblings, she spent her childhood alone reading and learning to sight-read music.

After countless failed attempts to encourage her to join in with local social activities – Wood loathed being bossed about and avoided 'joining in' anything like the plague – her sister Rosalind convinced her to enrol in a new arts education initiative in the neighbouring town of Rochdale. Spurred on by a mentor and sup-ported by a small group of actors and like-minded performers, Wood thrived. 'Workshop', as she called it, became the place where she came out of her shell. There, she would collaborate, try her hand at improv, bounce ideas off people, write and build her confidence as a singer, songwriter and performer. Victoria Wood OBE became one of the most loved and celebrated British entertainers of her generation.[16] Nominated for fourteen BAFTAs, she went on to sell out London's Royal Albert Hall 40 times.[17]

Wood had a solo act and was a deeply private perfectionist – but she didn't work in isolation. Her writing was forged by her audience, her collaborators and her peers. Her talent flourished because of other people. The major turning points in her career came when she formed creative partnerships with others; when she joined 'workshop' as a teenager and found her voice; when she built her resilience touring with fellow comedian John Dowie; when she was spotted by TV producer Peter Eckersley, who became a friend, advocate and mentor, when she married Geoffrey Durham, who pushed her towards stand-up and shaped her act; and when she met actor Julie Walters, who took her work in new directions – the list goes on.

Wood established a complex network of people to help and support her career over her life. She developed writing partnerships, joined groups (albeit kicking and screaming) and formed close bonds with others.

Always remember that how you work with, for and among other people will change across your life. Early on, you might need to find groups of people who give you the encouragement, support and feedback you need to keep going. Later on, you might need peers to support you. They will all play a role.

● ● ●

Nobel Prize-winning social scientist Gary Becker said that the most addictive thing on the planet isn't crack cocaine, Coca-Cola or caffeine – it's 'other people'.[18] Why? Because we need people more than anything else in the world. However private, introverted, controlling or shy a writer may be – other people make the difference. Whether you compete against them, collaborate with them or work with them in a way that spurs you on, other people will play a vital role – but how they do is up to you. It's time to figure out your accountability type and based on that, try out a few methods you can use to keep writing. Let's play in the Writer's Sandbox for the penultimate time.

The Writer's Sandbox – People

1. FIGURE OUT YOUR ACCOUNTABILITY TYPE

By now, you might have a hunch about what accountability type you are. Here's a quick recap of the two types:

Internal expectations: When you feel primarily accountable to yourself, you tend to meet your personal goals easily and you don't really need other people spurring you on.

External expectations: When you feel primarily accountable to others, you tend to put other people's needs above your own. You also find it tough to follow through with new plans and regimes without other people's help and support.

Remember that both these personality types have pros and cons (and neither are 'bad' nor 'good').

2. QUESTIONS TO EXPLORE YOUR TYPE

Primarily motivated by internal expectations? You might not need writing groups, but you could need help finding your 'why'. Do you delay starting things until you've understood them 100 per cent? That's another sign you could be more internally focussed.

Primarily motivated by external expectations? If your writing suffers because you constantly put others' needs above your own, that's a signal you're externally focussed.

Motivated by both? When you have double the expectation you can often end up feeling too busy as you try to meet your own personal goals and the demands everyone else puts on you.

Once you're clearer about your type, you can start designing an accountability system that helps you get the writing done.

3. IF YOU'RE MORE MOTIVATED BY INTERNAL EXPECTATIONS...

Start with why

Like the writer Simon Sinek's famous TED Talk and book – starting with 'why' can inspire greatness. Understanding why you are doing something and aligning your actions with your personal values, ambitions and goals is a powerful motivator. This approach is particularly effective if you have a tendency like Chris and need to understand why you're doing something before you commit to it.

Set a goal

Having a clear goal gives you something to aim for. As well as knowing what success looks like, break the goal into small steps and set milestones to monitor progress. Setting a small goal helps you build motivation and momentum and stops you from overthinking and delaying.

Meet a personal challenge

NaNoWriMo attracts hundreds of thousands of writers each year to write a 50,000-word novel in November. Bec found that having an ambitious goal can be incredibly effective – what about you? Challenges motivate us to stretch ourselves beyond what we're capable of. All you need to do is set a target just beyond your comfort zone – for some it might be the infamous Big Hairy Audacious Goal; for others it might be a simple practice such as maintaining a writing streak for as long as they can.

Collaborate

You might not need external accountability to keep you writing, but we all still benefit from writing with others. If you're primarily motivated by internal expectations, this can lead to you becoming a little too introspective (Chris says guilty as charged), which means that you can lose perspective and can sometimes get bogged down. Co-authoring relationships can help you bounce ideas off people and can make the whole writing experience a less intense, more enjoyable experience. Remember to consider the type of communal environment that works for you – do you thrive in collaborative or competitive situations? Are you motivated by 'winning' or is taking part enough?

Get yourself a writing tracker

When you're motivated by personal goals, seeing your progress build up over time is a great way to stay motivated. Log your progress in a way that works for you – go old-school with a paper diary or wall calendar, or use one of the plethora of apps that help you monitor your progress and streaks.

4. IF YOU'RE MORE MOTIVATED BY EXTERNAL EXPECTATIONS…

Go public

Psychologist Dr Gail Matthews from the Dominican University of California found that people who share their goals with a friend and send them weekly updates on progress are on average 33 per cent more successful in accomplishing them.[19] So, just tell people! It's surprising how many people embark on a writing project in secret. Just telling one other person – and asking them to check in on you regularly – is a great way to keep you moving forward.

Work with a writing buddy

There are many ways to work with a writing partner and the arrangement you choose can be formal or informal. One idea is to give the partnership some structure by signing a writers' 'contract', an actual signed agreement between two parties committing the writer to write on specific days. Another suggestion is to form a critiquing partnership where you share your writing and get feedback and offer guidance and support.

Join a writing group

Joining a writing group takes the critiquing partnership up a level. Groups vary in size and can be either online or face to face. The format can be different too. Some, like the Shut Up & Write! meetups we heard about earlier, work because they offer mutual support and encouragement – without judgement. Others are effective *because* of the peer support and feedback they provide. Investigate the meetups in your area and online, and decide whether you want to share your work with others or whether you'd just prefer the motivational push of working among other writers.

Get feedback from friends and family

It can be scary sharing your work with strangers, so some writers call on friends and family to read and offer feedback. The relationship is already in place, so you need to make sure they're clear what they are being asked to do and why. Ask specific questions, give them deadlines, and tell them how you want them to comment.

Find a writing coach or mentor

Having a coach or mentor can be pricey, but by working with a professional you get tailored advice and expertise to keep you on track. A good coach will respond to your needs and support you as you write. However, it's not an easy ride – you must do the work and they will hold you to account if you fail to meet your promise.

10,000 hours

DELIBERATE PRACTICE

3Fs

 FOCUS

 FEEDBACK

 FIX IT

CHAPTER 10

KEEP GOING

10

MASTERY

Forget talent – get better with time, feedback and deliberate practice

A few miles from where we now write in West Yorkshire, there once lived a clergyman and his family. 'The children lived in isolation in a parsonage high on the Yorkshire moors, which is to say, at the edge of the world,' wrote Joyce Carol Oates; 'each was possessed of an extraordinarily fecund imagination.'[1]

Those children were the Brontës – Charlotte, Emily, Anne and their brother, Patrick Branwell. After their mother and two eldest sisters died, the remaining four siblings were kept at home, an imposing hilltop parsonage. While it is easy to dramatise the hardship of these now-motherless children, they spent a lot of their early childhood reading, exploring the surrounding countryside and inventing stories based around a box of twelve wooden toy soldiers given to them by their father. Playing with the soldiers was their literary sandbox. What started out as childish storytelling games developed over many years into complex interwoven sagas and a series of tiny handwritten books inspired by periodicals of the time. As adults, the Brontë sisters shook the world of literature with their groundbreaking novels and poetry.

While Oates cautions us to not reduce the mature works of a poet or novelist to mere games, she argues that a writer's origins can be found in a child's dreaming mind. 'The imagination is expansive enough to accommodate both the child's fantasies and the strata-gems of the adult.'

That was certainly the case for Oates. Several academic arti-cles on developing writing skills refer to her youthful practice techniques, where she imitated the works of famous writers such as Hemingway. She wrote her novels in longhand and when one was completed she'd turn the pages over to write another. Oates describes this as: 'consciously training myself by writing novel after novel and always throwing them out when I completed them'.[2]

While Oates's juvenilia ended up in the bin, many of the books created by the Brontës survived. Over the years, scholars have taken their magnifying glasses to the minute, matchbox-sized volumes to explore the development of the Brontës as writers. Many have asked how these three sisters became such towering talents. Were they prodigies possessed of a precocious natural talent or did they work hard, practise and learn? Analysing their work and how they approached it, we can map how their storytelling games led to mas-tery. What's more, the Brontës' approach to practice can be applied to our own writing. Let's start at the beginning with how children learn to write.

LEARNING TO WRITE: FROM LABELS TO 'I LOVE YOU'

Children pick up writing early in life; three-year-olds can 'scrib-ble with a purpose'.[3] They recognise written words and understand that print carries a message. Research from the US Department of Education found that children can identify signs and labels, as well as recognising significant letters such as the initials of their own names, before they start school. By the time they're four years old, most pre-schoolers can attempt to write letters that represent lan-guage, especially for meaningful words like their names or phrases such as 'I love you'.

'That's the beginning of a two-decade-long process of developing writing skills. According to researcher Ronald T. Kellogg, there are three stages:[4]

1. **Knowledge telling:** writing for pleasure and play.
2. **Knowledge transforming:** writing for an audience.
3. **Knowledge crafting:** writing and editing for publication.

Bright students at school and college will master the first two stages. The final stage, however, is the preserve of mature adults who aim to become professional writers. Let's look at what this meant for the Brontë sisters as they moved through each stage.

1. Writing for pleasure and play

Play was the foundation of the Brontës' writing development – and what's more, the Brontës played for themselves alone. Together, the siblings wrote and performed plays with no audiences and produced magazines and books with no readers.[5] That's the most basic form of writing, what Kellogg calls 'knowledge telling', where the writing merely 'retrieves what the author wants to say and then generating a text to say it'.[6] To develop, the writer must move beyond egocentric writing to address readers.

2. Writing for an audience

Enter the Young Men, or the Twelves as the wooden toy soldiers were known. The Brontës were given the soldiers in June 1826 and soon grew attached to them, giving each soldier a name. While much has been made of the children's isolation, they always looked outward, avidly reading about discoveries in foreign countries. In December 1827 they wrote about Glass Town, an imaginary African kingdom, the first of what would become complex sagas.

The soldiers were the Brontës' first 'readers', the diminutive books the perfect size for the figurines. At this stage, the Brontës were entering Kellogg's second phase of writing development, called 'knowledge transforming', where there is both an understanding of an audience and a need to rework text, 'changing what the author wants to say as a result'.

The children's books increased in sophistication to include maps and illustrations of landscapes and buildings. They planned, reviewed and edited their work, working collaboratively to create the stories. This phase of invention stopped in 1834; perhaps some sibling rivalry fractured the creative partnership, they exhausted the imaginative potential, or merely grew too old to play with soldiers?[7] They continued writing and produced hundreds of short stories, plays, poems and novellas for many years before being published.

3. Writing and editing for publication

All this work honing their craft would take the Brontës into the final stage of writer development, that of 'knowledge crafting'. As a writer progresses to a level of professional expertise, they shape 'what they want to say and how to say it with the potential reader fully in mind'. And so, the sisters reached the milestone of expertise: publication. In 1846 a collection of poetry was published pseudonymously by Currer (Charlotte), Ellis (Emily), and Acton (Anne) Bell. While it might have had a reader in mind, it was not a success – just two copies were sold in its first year.* Over the following year the sisters worked on separate projects, writing alone but

---

* The same year the Brontës published their poetry, their father Patrick Brontë underwent eye surgery (without anaesthetic). As unmarried daughters of a clergyman, they were financially dependent on their father; when he died they would lose their home and income. It's important to note that the sisters were under significant pressure and that they were looking to make a living from writing. Their literary

discussing their writing for hours at the dinner table each night. In 1847, Charlotte's *Jane Eyre*, Emily's *Wuthering Heights*, and Anne's *Agnes Grey* were all published.

While the mythology of overnight success has the sisters exploding onto the literary scene, in reality it took twenty years from first playing at being authors, editors and publishers to become the writers they were destined to be.[8] Those two decades match exactly the time frame Kellogg says it takes to become an expert writer. While you might find this a tad dispiriting – you shouldn't. The Brontës weren't prodigies – they were grafters. Whether you're starting out today or have been writing for decades, you have the potential to become expert, if you're prepared to practise.

PRACTISE DELIBERATELY

Let's revisit the myth of the 'solitary genius'. In the last chapter we argued that writers need other people; now we're getting to the genius part of that phrase, ably assisted by psychologist K. Anders Ericsson, whose research on deliberate practice shows us how to shape our potential. Ericsson quashed the notion that talent is some kind of gift, a persuasive and dangerous notion that has dominated for too long. Take the Ancient Greeks and their idea of the Muses. The nine daughters of Mnemosyne and Zeus were seen as the source of all knowledge and arts. Even great writers like Homer couldn't start writing without invoking the Muses – the very first lines of his epic poem the *Odyssey* call for their assistance in getting the story down. When one of the greatest poets of antiquity feels they need divine intervention, it's no wonder this myth persisted for so long. Science took on religion in the 19th century, but rather

---

ambitions had high stakes – it wasn't about fun and games. Sadly, only Charlotte lived long enough to see any success in writing. Their father outlived them all.

than offering hope, it replaced heavenly gods with mortal ones: the ruling class. Eminent Victorians ascribed genius to a hereditary trait, gathering dodgy evidence to support their privilege and allowing them to entrench their dominant place in society and the arts.

Thankfully, Ericsson's more rigorous evidence supports an optimistic and equitable view of how talent develops. With nearly 300 publications, based on tens of studies across multiple domains, his findings transformed our understanding of human potential. 'That revolution starts,' said Ericsson, 'when we realize that the best among us in various areas do not occupy that perch because they were born with some innate talent but rather because they have developed their abilities through years of practice.'[9] His research on deliberate practice demonstrates that our growth is not limited, that our bodies and brains can adapt, and that through training we can create skills that did not exist before. In addition, we can keep developing these skills as we get older and spend more time working on them. Deliberate practice offers us a path to expertise at any age. While it's good to know that we don't need to be blessed by birthright or visited by the gods, therein lies the rub: it takes years to get really good at something. Which is why many of us give up long before we get good.

Ericsson's work builds on the 10-Year Rule, a concept that first emerged in a 1973 article looking at chess.[10] Since then it has been reproduced in multiple studies and domains, from music to mathematics and pretty much every sport played. One of his studies looking at violinists concluded that expertise requires several thousand hours of practice. On the plus side, there were no prodigies.[11] However, there were also no shortcuts. He found that those who had spent significantly more hours practising their craft were, on average, more accomplished than those who had spent less time practising. This study led to the popularisation of the 10,000-Hour

Rule, notably featured in Malcolm Gladwell's *Outliers: The Story of Success.*

Gladwell used the example of the Beatles playing in dingy backroom bars in Hamburg in the early 1960s to illustrate the rule. Over 1,200 gigs, they amassed more than 10,000 hours of performance time and transformed themselves into the most popular band of their era. But it's not a simple equation. Hours of practice doesn't guarantee success. As Paul McCartney said after reading *Outliers*: 'There were an awful lot of bands that were out in Hamburg who put in 10,000 hours and didn't make it, so it's not a cast-iron theory. However, when you look at a group who has been successful ... you always will find that amount of work in the background.'[12]

McCartney is right. You need to practise – that goes without saying – but to become an expert, and for that to lead to success, you need to do more than rack up the hours. Gladwell's book might have topped the bestsellers' chart and been critically applauded, but Ericsson felt he overemphasised the 10,000-Hour Rule. In essence, practice matters, but *how* you practise matters more.

NOT ALL PRACTICE IS THE SAME

At the most basic level there's 'naïve' practice – literally just showing up and doing the activity again and again. We heard in Chapter 8 that 43 per cent of our daily lives is spent performing habitual tasks – this shortcut enables us to get through the day with ease. For many people, tasks like cooking or exercising are about practising automatic behaviours. That's fine if all we need to do is eat and move, but if you want to be a chef or a competitive sportsperson, you need to step up to 'purposeful' practice.

Ericsson describes purposeful practice as such: 'Get outside your comfort zone but do it in a focused way, with clear goals, a plan for reaching those goals, and a way to monitor your progress. Oh, and figure out a way to maintain your motivation.'[13]

An example of Ericsson's purposeful practice would be a writing workshop. If you sign up for 'Write a Short Story in a Weekend', you have a clear goal. The structure of the course provides a plan for achieving that goal with support from an experienced tutor. You can monitor your progress with words on the page as you do each of the timed exercises. Working in a group keeps you motivated, often with a sense of competition, especially when you add in the pressure of writing against the clock. At the end of the weekend, you have completed a short story. That's what Stephanie Scott thought when she first signed up for a weekend writing historical fiction. Writing a short story, her first ever, changed Scott's life. Up until that point, she'd never written creatively. Back in 2010 she was a rising star in investment banking and engaged to be married. She signed up for the course as a fun way to spend a weekend; she ended up quitting her job to write full time, working on a novel for ten years. She provides a template for deliberate practice – but before we explore that, we need to go back to that first workshop.

Writing workshops are brilliant at teaching us the fundamentals. However, studies have found that while watching lectures or attending courses might increase knowledge, they don't lead to any improvement in skill. In short, to become a good writer you have to practise that skill and get expert feedback to improve your performance. Scott's tutor that weekend spotted potential in that early draft and encouraged Scott to apply for a place on a novel-writing course at Faber Academy. Scott dutifully edited the short story and sent it off with her application, and at the same time applied for a Masters in creative writing at the University of Oxford – again sending off her one and only story. She won places at both, resigned from work, a week later she got married and the very next day (with confetti still in her hair) she was back in student accommodation, her husband smuggled into the single room with her. That was just the beginning of her practice.

Now, naïve or purposeful practice is enough to write a short story, but to write a *good* short story, you need to get deliberate. Ericsson found that to hit the top level of practice, we must swap fun for struggle, sacrifice and painful self-assessment. We need to go beyond the weekend course and commit to the long haul. He tells us that to become an expert, to focus 'on tasks beyond your current level of competence and comfort, you will need a well-informed coach not only to guide you through deliberate practice but also to help you learn how to coach yourself'.[14] That weekend writing course gave Scott all three of those things: she was working on a new skill beyond her current ability, she met a coach who would 'midwife' her novel, and it gave her a model of how to identify areas of craft that needed development. However, the first thing she needed to do was give it time. Lots of time.

Let's see how Scott emulated the elements of deliberate practice. The first element is that it took ten years from her first short story in 2010 to the publication of her debut novel in 2020 – the 'rule' at the heart of Ericsson's work. This chapter has bandied around a lot of time frames. Not only is there the 10-Year Rule, there's also Kellogg's concept that it takes twenty years to develop expert writing skills. Thankfully, these are concurrent not additional – the 10-Year Rule fits within the final phase of Kellogg's writer development, and his research draws significantly on Ericsson's with specific application to writing.

As famous as he is for the 10-Year Rule, Ericsson is less attached to a specific number of hours or years, saying 'take the time you need', though don't expect any quick wins.[15] While Scott knew it would take her a long time, she didn't bank on it being quite so long. She'd originally saved enough money to be able to give up work, but the money wouldn't last forever, so she set herself until the end of her Masters course to decide whether to continue writing or go back to full-time paid employment. 'You have to set boundaries,' Scott told us, 'give yourself time to make a decision and see if it works for you.'

At the end of the MA, Scott received positive indications that she should continue. She entered numerous UK writing competitions and had success on shortlists and winning prizes. That provided feedback that she was getting better – an essential part of deliberate practice. A significant boost came when she won the A.M. Heath Prize for New Writing and the prize money enabled her to keep going. For many of us, financing our writing is a limiting factor, so getting additional support from The National Centre For Writing, as well as research funding from the Toshiba Foundation and the British Association of Japanese Studies for a trip to Japan, where her novel is set, made all the difference.

'No one is an overnight success,' said Scott. 'It looks like you burst onto the stage fully formed, but of course, there's several years where you are forming. I put a lot of time into developing craft.' Her work on craft gets us into the nuts and bolts of deliberate practice.

HOW TO PRACTISE DELIBERATELY

There are two types of learning involved in deliberate practice: improving the skills you have and extending the reach and range of your skills. Many people are taught to write at school, and this decade or so of learning sets up the foundational skills. That is more than adequate for everyday life, but to master expertise, writers need to keep working at their writing. Formal writing courses have been in place for many decades, and while social media likes to debate whether writing can be taught, the research shows it can.

Ericsson goes so far as to claim that the highest levels of expertise are not possible without access to training, the formal organisation of knowledge, activity and expertise.[16]

In her early training, Scott kept extending the reach and range of her writing skills. 'Focussing on craft and developing my writing skillset has been invaluable to my progression as a writer, as has the opportunity to write across genres.' She's right – writers need different teachers at different stages and for different skills. For many of us, we start with local teachers, perhaps a class in a nearby bookshop, college or library. As we progress towards expertise we seek out more advanced teachers to keep improving our skills. As Ericsson found, 'eventually, all top performers work closely with teachers who have themselves reached international levels of achievement'.[17] With writing courses now firmly established in the UK, you can shortcut this route by learning from world-class writers. Bec managed residential writing courses for Arvon, an educational charity that has taught writing at historical rural houses in the UK for over 50 years. It was there, in our hometown, down the road from where the Brontës lived, that she first met Scott in 2013. While thousands came through the doors, Scott stood out because she'd booked two courses, in completely different disciplines, back to back, which seemed a rather weird thing to do. It makes sense now: she was pushing her skills as a novelist by exploring poetry and writing for radio.

GETTING BETTER WITH COACHES AND MENTORS

To get the full value of working with experts, the emphasis has to be on individual feedback. Ericsson found that real experts are motivated to seek out coaches and mentors who can provide constructive, even painful feedback. Coaches accelerate the learning process and are the final component for developing expertise. While short courses are great for a boost, they are no substitute for working with a dedicated coach and building a relationship that provides a safe space for the kind of constructive feedback that is necessary to grow as a writer. Scott had two long-term coaches, both of whom she met via the courses she took. 'It is key,' she said, 'for every young writer to have a mentor whose expertise and judgement they trust.'

Trust is central to the coach-student relationship because of the nature of the feedback. Ericsson found that elite performers have to be unsentimental, picking coaches who 'would challenge them and drive them to higher levels of performance'.[18] This all comes back to mindset and the importance of being non-judgemental. Scott says her coaches never pulled their punches. 'Being kind,' she explains, 'is the last thing you need! I'm very lucky to work with people where it's just about the craft. I mean, we're really good friends and we love each other very much. But when you're talking about what's on the page, it's just on the page.'

A good coach will train the writer to coach themselves; this is what Ericsson calls having 'mental representations', the ability to anticipate feedback. Scott describes it like this: 'There is a point where you leave your mentor. You can be friends and keep in touch, but there's a point where you step up on your own.'

For Scott this meant hunkering down to write. 'I stopped with the learning and the courses. I just went into my cave. I think I'd built up enough expertise by that point. I was totally self-editing and judging my own craft by that point.' Scott's cave is her metaphorical place where she practised her skills as a writer. She worked alone to put into practice all she had learnt on courses and from her mentors. Learning from those more advanced than you is a vital component of mastery, but as the research shows, courses alone are not sufficient; you must practise. Self-coaching offers a process for doing this.

On to the final stage of mastery, which thankfully doesn't cost anything (apart from blood, sweat and tears).

HOW TO COACH YOURSELF

The most famous example of self-coaching is that of Benjamin Franklin, one of the Founding Fathers of the United States, a polymath with expertise in science, diplomacy and the arts. In his autobiography, he recounts his early life and love of reading as a child – when any money came his way he spent it on books. He followed his 'bookish inclination' and started working at a printer in his teens, all the while nurturing his ambition to write.

In what must have been a mortifying incident in his youth, Franklin recalls when his father found letters he'd written to a friend. Unprompted, his father fed back, cuttingly, that while his spelling was correct, 'I fell far short in elegance of expression, in method and in perspicuity, of which he convinced me by several instances. I saw the justice of his remarks, and thence grew more attentive to the manner in writing, and determined to endeavour at improvement.'[19]

Rather than enlist his father as a coach (a decision highly relatable to any teenager), Franklin learned how to self-coach. He wrote at night after a day at work, early mornings before his shift began, or on Sunday when he avoided going to church – prioritising his writing over worship. His initial inspiration came from the *Spectator*, a political journal from London, which gave him a model of good writing to emulate. 'I thought the writing excellent, and wished, if possible, to imitate it.'

He developed a process of reading, copying, working from memory, and even rewriting articles in verse before turning them back into prose. Throughout, he referred back to the original text. 'By comparing my work afterwards with the original,' wrote

Franklin, 'I discovered many faults and amended them; but I sometimes had the pleasure of fancying that, in certain particulars of small import, I had been lucky enough to improve the method or the language, and this encouraged me to think I might possibly in time come to be a tolerable English writer, of which I was extremely ambitious.'

Franklin's process of improving his writing skills is a masterclass in self-coaching. 'To effectively practice a skill without a teacher,' writes Ericsson, 'it helps to keep in mind three Fs: Focus. Feedback. Fix it. Break the skill down into components that you can do repeatedly and analyze effectively, determine your weaknesses, and figure out ways to address them.'[20] Practising is not about just sitting down and writing, and it's interesting that Franklin didn't compose original articles. This is the mistake that many of us make as writers – focussing on practice time rather than practising in a deliberate way. That's why the over-emphasis on time, racking up your 10,000 hours, is so misleading. This approach to practice can feel frustrating – Franklin worked on the same articles over and over again; it's doubtful he ever had a final version. Though it sounds like he enjoyed the process he created for learning – it's playful to turn political articles into poetry – the point of this exercise was not to produce a poem but to extend his skills. This is what Scott was doing by attending different courses back to back. While her core focus was writing a novel, she wanted to learn more about other forms of writing. She explains:

'Reading and writing poetry can be extremely beneficial when in search of rigour and attention to detail in your own writing. Similarly, just as drama is admired for its wit and brevity, learning how playwrights develop plot and emotional relationships using only dialogue can be instrumental when working on one's own dramatic scenes in prose. Experimenting with form will teach you a lot about your work, what you want to create and what you want to achieve.'

Her study of poetry and playwriting might have looked like procrastination to her friends and family who repeatedly asked why she wasn't working on her novel, but it was all part of her process of becoming a writer. When her novel *What's Left of Me Is Yours* was published in 2020, critics from the *Wall Street Journal*, the *Guardian*, the *New York Times* and the *Daily Mail* praised her exquisite and sensuous writing, saying that not only was it a stunning debut, but that it had the skills of a master beyond her age. It took years of practice for Scott to master writing, for her to work deliberately on the skills she needed to produce a critically acclaimed novel that has not only been shortlisted for numerous prizes but is much loved by readers the world over.

As Ericsson writes: 'And this, more than anything else is the lesson that people should take away from all these stories and all this research: There is no reason not to follow your dream. Deliberate practice can open the door to a world of possibilities that you may have been convinced were out of reach. Open that door.'[21]

If you scratch the surface of any writer's success you will find years of practice underneath. Research shows that if people keep writing in a purposeful and deliberate way they will continue to improve. At any age. As the Chinese proverb states: 'The best time to plant a tree was twenty years ago. The second-best time is today.' The following exercises take you through the process of developing mastery. They might not speed up the process of becoming an expert performer, but they will help you practise your skills deliberately and make the best use of your writing time. Remember that every time you write, if you do it in a deliberate and mindful way, you'll get better. Today's practice will make you a better writer than you were yesterday, last week, last year. Embrace 'second-best' by starting today and keeping going.

The Writer's Sandbox – Mastery

1. WRITE AND REVISE WITH THE READER IN MIND

Ronald T. Kellogg outlines the three stages of writer development from knowledge telling, to knowledge transforming, and finally knowledge crafting, where the writer shapes what they want to say and how to say it with the reader fully in mind. The Brontës wrote for their toy soldiers; you can start writing for a made-up audience so you understand meaning from their perspective.[22] Another approach is to create a persona, a composite personality used in marketing and product development.

It can be difficult to read your own writing because you are often too close to it to get perspective. Researchers suggest imagining a reader while editing, 'whose existence and whose expectations influence their revision process'.[23] To step into someone else's shoes and gain valuable external perspective, write a reader's name on a piece of paper near your writing desk or ask: *'What would [insert name] think?'* so you can write for them.

Creating distance can aid objectivity, stopping you feeling too attached to the darlings you are about to kill. It's one reason why many authors put their work in a drawer and ignore it for weeks; putting your work aside gives you much-needed perspective.

2. GET DELIBERATE AS YOU PRACTISE

There are different elements to deliberate practice, which draw on some of the themes in this book. These include:

Drive: the intrinsic motivation to engage in the task.

Effort: working hard to improve performance.

Stretch: practising close to the edge of your current level of ability.

Feedback: to get knowledge of your progress and results.

Repeat: high levels of task repetition.

Rather than get distracted by the amount of time, the frequency or regularity of writing, focus on how you spend that time. That means getting deliberate.

According to Anders Ericsson, the hallmark of deliberate practice 'is that you try to do something you cannot do – that takes you out of your comfort zone – and that you practice it over and over again, focusing on exactly how you are doing it, where you are falling short, and how you can get better'.[24] Be warned, Ericsson described it as high on effort and low on enjoyment, but the rewards from seeing your progress will offset the short-term pain.

3. FIND A MENTOR OR BECOME YOUR OWN COACH

If you've read the previous chapter you'll have a good idea about how people can help and what sort of support you might benefit from. There are mentors for all sorts of writers and for all aspects of the writing and editing process, though it can be expensive. Longer term, you need to emulate Benjamin Franklin and learn to coach yourself.

Follow the three Fs: Focus, Feedback, Fix it. That all starts by identifying areas to develop – these can be short and long term. Observe your writing skills, break the skill into components so you can analyse what is going on, find areas that can be improved, and experiment with ways to address them. Start by using our questions for reflection at the end of every writing session:

- ↤ What went well?
- ↤ What didn't go so well?
- ↤ What will I do differently next time?

4. DON'T WORK FOR TOO LONG

Another trap people fall into with the 10,000-Hours Rule is to simply rack up the hours, assuming longer writing sessions are the way to go. The research shows that shorter, more focussed sessions are far better. While there is no consensus on what the ideal length of session is (after all, productivity is personal), the research suggests anything from one hour up to four hours is possible for a cognitively demanding task like writing.[25]

Once you build a regular writing routine, you may find that you can increase the length of time you are able to focus. It might start quite small, just ten or fifteen minutes, but as you practise you could reach a few hours of flow. Observe how long you can focus for, how you feel, and experiment by extending the sessions little by little.

5. TAKE A BREAK, HAVE A NAP, SLEEP!

Ericsson discovered an interesting link between the number of practice hours and the number of hours spent sleeping each week. The 'best' students he studied 'averaged around five hours more of sleep than the good students, mostly by taking more time for afternoon naps'. Taking time off is as valuable as time spent practising, as long as it is done with intention.

Don't underestimate how important rest is. Other studies found that once writers had completed their allocated session, they 'spend the rest of the day on walking, correspondence, napping, and other less demanding activities'.[26] When the writing is done give yourself a break.

6. KEEP GOING – YOU ARE GETTING BETTER

Every year you write, as long as you practise deliberately, you will get better. Bestselling non-fiction writer Geoff Colvin found that: 'Many scientists and authors produce their greatest work only after twenty or so years of devoted effort, which means in year nineteen they are still getting better.'[27]

● ● ●

One of our guilty pleasures (which might reveal a little about our own age), is reading about writers who were published later in life. This isn't a recent phenomenon. Daniel Defoe published his first long work of fiction, *Robinson Crusoe*, in 1719 when he was 59. Laura Ingalls Wilder published her first book, *Little House in the Big Woods*, in 1932 when she was 65 years old. There are many later-life emerging writers, from Toni Morrison (39), to Raymond Chandler (51), Mary Wesley (57 for children's books and 71 for her adult novels), Frank McCourt (66) and Millard Kaufman (90). So much so, that Bec's dream is to enter her first (as yet unwritten novel) in the Royal Society of Literature's Christopher Bland Prize for a debut writer first published aged 50 or over. As Bland himself said, 'I started the creative life at the age of 76, so it's never too late.'

CONCLUSION

The quantity myth

This final chapter was a struggle for us to write. We wrestled with it for months. At one point it was the first chapter in the book. Then we cut it and put some of it in the Introduction. Then it appeared somewhere in the middle. People read early drafts and gave us helpful feedback, but much of it was conflicting, as feedback often is. It was up to us to figure things out – slowly, over time and with lots of tea, head-scratching and dog walks. Is it right now? Who knows? And what does 'right' mean anyway?

Enough with this self-indulgent navel-gazing! you might cry. *What does this matter to me?* But the point is this: you can never really know whether the end product of your creative endeavours will be any good or not. When you're knee-deep in it, it can feel like you've got all the parts strewn around you like bits of an engine you're trying to assemble. You can never know for certain whether you can make it work or not, or whether the end result will be an embarrassing flop or a game-changing success. Imagine if you did know! Imagine if you knew for certain which ideas, conclusions or stories your readers would love and which they'd loathe. All the effort you'd save. You'd know which part to put where.

But of course, you can't know any of this. The very nature of the creative process is full of blind alleys, faint lights at the end of the tunnel, false starts and handbrake turns. But while you'll never be able to accurately predict the outcome of your writing efforts, you do have the power to do one very important thing.

CREATIVE HITS AND MISSES

One of the most common attributes of creative people, says psychologist Dean Keith Simonton, is that they are extraordinarily poor at judging whether the thing they're writing or creating at the time will be a hit or a miss. And when they do feel sure, they invariably get it wrong. In one paper he analyses the output of some of the world's most successful and famous classical composers. He writes about Handel, who pinned all his hopes on a few operas that he loved but everyone else loathed. Then there's Beethoven, who predicted incorrectly time and time again which of his compositions would be most popular. Simonton found that the group of composers he studied were hopeless at predicting which of their pieces were going to be masterworks or mistakes. Success wasn't linked to how much effort (or not) a composer may have put into a particular piece of work, or how quickly (or not) they had dashed it off. Many of the pieces that they'd toiled over for years sank without trace, while many of the pieces they were perhaps least proud of went on to be huge hits. 'When a composer condescends to produce a rash of "pot boilers" or "pièces d'occasion" for monetary or promotional gains, the production of masterpieces is not sacrificed,' writes Simonton. 'This finding raises the issue of whether the creative genius has much capacity to discern between major and minor works. Evidently, only posterity can make the final judgment.'[1] And not only that, his research found no specific patterns as to when these composers reached their creative peak. Some had huge successes early on, then experienced long barren periods followed by big wins at the end of their lives. Others produced classics like clockwork throughout their lives.

In a later study, Simonton goes on to write about the hits and misses of inventor Thomas Edison who registered a mammoth 1,093 patents over a 64-year career.[2] While Edison is known for world-changing inventions like the light bulb and the telephone, he also registered patents for rather less world-changing ones. Like a peculiar talking 'phonograph doll' (google it, we promise it will freak you out), the 'spirit phone' (for chatting to ghosts, of course) and the electric pen. Powered by an acid-filled battery, the Edison Pen was a cast-iron 'perforation' device about the size of a small suitcase. While it didn't catch on for writing, the patent was bought by a tattoo artist who adapted the machine to perforate his clients. In the end, Edison's pen lost out to the smaller and distinctly less hazardous typewriter a few years later. While the inventor might have had a hunch that some of the gadgets he was inventing were going to be more successful than others, he can't have been certain at the time. It's likely that he hoped they'd all take off and applied the same vim and vigour to the creation of each.

Simonton studied the work and lives of hundreds of famous writers, scientists, inventors, artists and musicians to see if they had any common attributes and whether creative genius could be predicted in some way. He couldn't find much. There was no causal link between age and success that was common to all. While people in some disciplines had longer creative careers than others, age didn't preclude anyone from producing their best work.* Being

---

* In his research, Simonton calculates the 'half-life' of creatives working in different fields, that being the point at which a creative person has half their creative career remaining. For poets this was: 15.4 years, mathematicians: 21.7 years, novelists: 20.4 years, geologists: 28.9 years and historians 39.7 years. He writes: 'This latter observation may help in appreciating why poets actually have shorter life spans than do other literary figures ... Because they burn themselves out so fast, relatively speaking, poets may die younger without leaving as much potential creativity "nipped in the bud." In contrast, novelists and historians who die unusually young will have seen far less of their creative potential realized and thus may not yet have produced a sufficient quantity of outstanding work on which to hand a durable posthumous reputation.'[3]

old or young was neither a limitation nor an advantage. He examined whether external factors affected creativity and considered whether historical events had an impact. Again, he couldn't find many patterns. The people he studied kept creating at about the same rate in times of peace, war, abundance, famine, prosperity and recession. The only thing that stopped them is if they fell ill.

But saying all this, Simonton's conclusion wasn't that the factors which influence creative 'greatness' were random. He did find one thing that the most successful (or notorious) creatives often had in common. And doing this one thing will give you the best chance of success too – but sadly, it often has a bad reputation.

THE PRODUCTIVITY PREJUDICE

Brian Clegg is an internationally acclaimed author who has published 84 books: 24 business, 50 popular science and ten fiction. Although by now, he's probably written a few more. He has eclectic interests: quantum computing, murder mystery and climate science. A member of the Institute of Physics and the Royal Society, he also pops up on British TV now and again to explain complex scientific concepts in pithy plain English. Yet when we interviewed Clegg for our blog – at the time he was busy promoting his latest work, a book about Einstein called *Gravitational Waves* – a reviewer at *New Scientist* had just written this: 'Brian Clegg is such a prolific writer of popular science, it is easy to forget how good he is.' Tweeting out the reviewer's backhanded compliment, Clegg commented: 'Of course there is a danger that for writers, being productive can be considered a negative.' While undoubtedly the reviewer at the esteemed journal meant no offence, they probably weren't joking either. But to us, this throwaway line revealed a lot.

In this book you've heard us talk a lot about the myths we come to believe about how writing should and shouldn't be done.

We've written about how these myths crystallise over time and form dogma that influences how we behave. Now, we're going to tell you about the last and final myth of the book – it's what we call the 'quantity myth' – and we're going to turn to Adam Grant, one of the most prolific and high-profile academics in his field to explain. 'It's widely assumed there's a trade-off between quantity and quality,' he writes, 'that if you want to do better work you have to do less of it, but this turns out to be false. In fact, when it comes to idea generation, quantity is the most predictable path to quality.'[4]

This was Simonton's verdict too. His work found that productivity and quantity was the thing that made writers, artists and inventors great. Over four decades of research, Simonton found that the key factor to creative greatness wasn't innate talent, but rather how many books writers had written, how many research papers scientists had produced, how many films filmmakers had made, how many patents an inventor had filed, how many sonatas a composer had composed, how many times a performer had performed, and so on. Sure, some people will have more talent than others, but talent in itself doesn't lead to success. His research finds that the most successful creatives aren't necessarily more gifted than their less successful peers. Rather, they produce more, which improves their overall chances of having a hit. 'I must predict an intimate connection between quantity and quality,' concludes Simonton. 'Both good and bad ideas should appear throughout the career. Indeed, the odds of producing an influential or successful idea should be a positive function of the total number of ideas generated. Quality is then a probabilistic function of quantity.'[5] Contrary to the pervading quantity myth, creative geniuses don't become geniuses by narrowly working in one area, striving to produce one 'great work'; they cast the net widely and produce many things in the hope (but not the knowledge) that some might succeed.*

But why does this myth have such a hold on us? One reason is because we often have a false understanding about our creative potential. We have come to fear that our creative capacity might dry up or that having too many ideas makes those ideas progressively worse and of a lower quality. In fact, the opposite is true. To explain this further, let's return to the research into creative persistence which we touched on in the Introduction.

PERSISTENCE PAYS

In 2015, a team of social psychologists invited writers from 131 comedy groups to come up with as many funny endings as they could in four minutes to this scene opener: 'Four people are laughing hysterically on stage. Two of them high five and everyone stops laughing immediately and someone says___.' The research team were attending a festival called Sketchfest, a ten-day event hosting professional comedy writing troupes from around the United States. An example ending the researchers gave to the scene was: 'In this country high fives mean "orgy" – run!' or 'And that is how the Glue brothers became joined at the palm.' Cue hilarity or tumbleweed, depending on your sense of humour.

The researchers started the stopwatch and the sketch writers worked away. On average they wrote around six endings each. Pats on the back all round. But then the research team upped the ante.

---

* Research among every Nobel Prize-winner between 1901 and 2005 concludes that the individuals who are the most prestigious in their chosen fields are also the ones with the highest number and widest range of hobbies such as creative writing, poetry, performing, painting, singing or drawing. Contrary to what you might expect, less decorated scientists tend to have a far narrower focus and far fewer interests outside science.[6]

Could they do it again? If they were given another four minutes, would they produce fewer endings, about the same or more? Now, let's remember, these writers were comedy pros. Many had been on the international festival circuit for years. They'd written thousands of gags, been through the mill, heckled, applauded, booed – God knows what else – at events across the globe. You might assume that they knew what they were capable of, these hard-as-nails comics. You might not expect they'd get spooked at the idea of having to repeat a simple exercise for a few visiting boffins. But they all did. A lifetime of writing and performing still didn't stop these professionals from underestimating their capacity to keep coming up with new and original funny endings.

It wasn't a case of fake modesty or erring on the side of caution. As a group, these comics predicted that they'd come up with far fewer ideas than they actually did when the researchers started the stopwatch a second time. Over seven other similar tests, the research team asked other groups of people – writers, creatives, some professionals, some not – about how productive or creative they thought they could be given more time or more resources. All the tests confirmed that people often underestimate their creative capacities.

They underestimated how many ideas they could generate, they underestimated the speed at which they could generate ideas, they thought that the outcomes would be far worse and of far lower quality than they actually turned out to be, and they underestimated their ability to solve hard tasks as opposed to easy ones. Age and experience didn't matter. Creative professionals with years of experience in their field felt just as unsure about their potential as complete amateurs.

The problem, the researchers conclude, is that the trial-and-error nature of the creative process can lead to people quitting on their projects too early – and this can have some serious consequences. The psychologists warn us that the creative process can be so effortful – or using their term, causes so much 'disfluency' – that it can lead to people quitting on their projects altogether if they don't find a way to keep going. 'Undervaluing persistence may lead people to prematurely conclude their creative work and potentially leave their best ideas undiscovered,' they write.[7]

YOU DON'T KNOW HOW GOOD YOU ARE

Have you ever read *The Secret Diary of Adrian Mole, Aged 13¾* by Sue Townsend? It was one of Chris's favourite books growing up. He'd never read anything like it. It was funny, sweet and relatable. It helped him through some difficult times as a kid. He must have read it 100 times (that and *The Hitchhiker's Guide to the Galaxy*). But did you know that Townsend's book nearly never made it to the shelves because she thought the book wasn't worth the paper it was written on?

After she first came up with the idea for Adrian Mole, she wrote a few chapters of his diaries but then got disillusioned with the whole idea. That *what am I doing with my life?* stage might be famil-iar to you too. So, she stuffed the manuscript in a big cardboard box and assumed it would never see the light of day again. 'It joined twenty years' worth of bad poetry, unfinished short stories and song lyrics, mostly written in the small hours when the children were asleep,'[8] she said. At the time, Townsend had three jobs. By day, she worked as a community organiser and a youth worker, while in the evening she waited on tables at a bar. She was exhausted most of the time – but she continued writing. She joined a writing group to give her structure and accountability and submitted pieces now and again to regional writing competitions. She got rejections, picked herself up, dusted herself off and kept going. Eventually, she won an award. It was only a small regional prize, but suddenly doors creaked open. She got hired as a writer at a local theatre, which gave her a network and contacts. Producers and directors got interested in her writing. They began to ask: 'What are you working on next?' Realising at that point she didn't have anything original to give them, she remembered that old box stuffed full of half-finished work. She decided to fish out her Adrian Mole manuscripts – perhaps someone might be interested in this?

They were very interested. She was asked to submit a proposal but didn't have time, so she just sent the three chapters she had – probably thinking that was that. But slowly, word spread. One producer talked to another producer. The extracts got passed around and found their way to a publisher – who read them, loved them, and asked Townsend to write a book. So, that's what she did. But after all these ups and downs, successes and failures, she still felt mortified by her work. So mortified that when she first heard that her publisher was planning to publish 5,000 hardback copies of her first book, she phoned them and asked them not to print it: she thought it was rubbish and didn't think it would sell. Thankfully, her publisher at the time knew better. And we should all be very, very pleased they did. Today, *The Secret Diary of Adrian Mole* has sold well over 5 million copies and been translated into 45 languages. Townsend had talent, but she was only able to realise that talent because she kept going – she kept doing.

FIND THE THINGS ONLY YOU CAN DO

Being interviewed, the writer and tech guru Kevin Kelly explains that while editing the magazine he founded, he had something of an epiphany.[9] At *Wired*, around half the articles came from submissions (freelance journalists pitching ideas to him) while the other half came from commissions (Kelly pitching out ideas for journalists to write). The ideas for these assignments came from various places and often from Kelly. Sometimes he found it easy to commission out these assignments, while other times he struggled – really struggled. 'Often, I'd have an idea and I'd try to find a freelancer to give them the assignment – but I'd have no luck in selling the idea or even giving it away,' he explained. So, he'd just file the idea away and assume it wasn't a very good idea after all. Some of the ideas went away but others stuck with him. Year after year, knock-back after knock-back, he kept trying to convince reluctant journalists to run with his stories. *These ideas are so bad*, he must have thought, *I can't even pay someone to write about them*. But instead of giving up, he changed tack. He commissioned himself.

He set about writing the stories that nobody else wanted. Fully expecting these articles to flop, to his surprise, he found that these pieces made his magazine fly off the shelves. These articles became his best, most well-read, most career-defining work. And this was his epiphany: 'I was doing the things that only I could do,' he says. That's what made them good.

HOW TO GET IT WRITTEN

All well and good, you might think. *But how on earth do you know what it is that only you can do, make, create or write?* You keep going, that's how. You might think you will run out of good ideas – but you won't. You might think that you can't keep going – but you can. You might think your first idea is the best you'll ever have – but you'll always have more – and they will improve. Your creativity is boundless and your potential limitless – but you will only get to understand what it is that you can do if you keep making, keep producing, keep writing and keep creating.

We wrote this book with the sole purpose of helping you to keep going as a writer. But the ideas in it can guide your life. After all, our whole lives are trial and error strewn with highs and lows, ups and downs, breakthroughs and blocks. The more mindful you become about what you believe and how you live, the better you'll be able to weather the kind of 'disfluency' that can derail you and stop you from achieving your potential. 'Keep going' is easy to say but difficult to achieve in practice. Hopefully we've given you an approach and some tactics to know *how* to keep going and to become more resilient in the face of the inevitable bumps in the road that will occur over the course of your writing life and beyond.

Good things don't come to those who wait, they come to those who *do*. To those who put things out into the world and are open to experimentation.

So, whatever it is that you do, keep doing it.

Whatever it is you create, keep creating it.

Keep learning, keep experimenting, keep adapting, keep going.

Because in the end, that's the only thing we know for certain that really works.

TAKE THE NEXT STEP

Thank you for reading this book. Before you move on, take a moment to reflect. What have you noticed about yourself or your writing? What change are you going to make? What are you going to do differently?

Tell us – it might even help you do it. Email us at hello@ prolifiko.com

Talking of doing things, there's a few things you could do to support us:

- Leave a review. It helps other people find out about the book, and it will help us to understand what you liked and how we can do more to support other writers.
- Sign up to our newsletter *Breakthroughs and Blocks*. It's a friendly pep talk that keeps your inner critic in check and your doubts at bay. We'll send you new ideas to try, stories to inspire you and the latest research on behaviour change, psychology and writing. Sign up here: breakthroughsandblocks.substack.com
- Check our our latest courses and coaching at writtenacademy. com you can also follow us on Instagram @writtenacademy or on LinkedIn as Prolifiko where you can also connect with Bec and Chris.

Keep writing,
Bec and Chris

PS: Don't forget you can get all the downloads mentioned in this book by going to: **prolifiko.com/writtenresources**

ACKNOWLEDGEMENTS

You might recall that this book began with some words from scriptwriter Jimmy McGovern. Chris heard an interview with the writer while burning some toast on an uneventful morning in the summer of 2022. The words were these: *I don't love writing, but I love having written.* As we wrote in the footnote, while McGovern did say this, many other writers have said similar things. Now, we can say it too. What has helped – in fact, not just helped, but made this book possible – are other people. We wrote in Chapter 9 that this book is the product of two people – but in reality, it's the product of many more.

Firstly, we'd like to thank our agent Michael Alcock and the team at Johnson and Alcock along with everyone at Icon Books for their belief in the book, their patience, persistence and kindness and their ability to withstand Bec's organisational onslaughts. We'd particularly like to thank our editors Kiera Jamison and Hanna Milner.

Next, we'd like to say a huge thank you to Oliver Burkeman – both for his inspiring foreword and for being so generous with his limited time.

Working with Cara Holland and the team at Graphic Change on the original illustrations for the book has been an absolute delight. Thank you for bringing our words to life visually.

Early on, we worked with development editors Parul Bavishi and Randall Surles whose feedback on how to structure the book kept us focussed on craft and storytelling. We are indebted to

Caroline Curtis who read an early proof and gave feedback on the text, grammar and voice.

We'd like to say a huge thank you to everyone who we interviewed for the book – too many to mention here – for your patience with us and for believing in the project. Our beta readers helped us focus on what advice writers really need and their feedback throughout the writing process made *Written* better than it ever would have been. Thank you for your time, kindness and generosity. Our beta readers were: Angela Billows, Anna Giulia Phippen-Novero, Chris J L Allen, Edith A. Fadul, Jane Creaton, Jim Vander Putten, Jo Garrick, Jonathan O'Donnell, Kaushalya Perera, Kristin Kari Janke, Louise Bassett, M. Rose Barlow, Nicki Robson, Nina Fudge, Phil Harrison, Rani Elvire, Ruth Goldsmith, Sarah Breen, Simon Linacre, Sue Burkett, Sundeep Aulakh and Trina Garnett.

As is the case when writing a mammoth project like a book, we couldn't have done it without the help, support and encouragement of friends and family. Starting with our mums, everlasting gratitude to Carol Evans and Joyce Smith. This book is dedicated to our dads, Richard Evans and Colin Smith, who would be so proud of us. Bec's siblings; Matthew, Imogen, Dominic and Tristan; their partners Dee, Matt and Jane; and our niblings Harriet, Daniel, Ellis, Eric, Ruby and Olive – the future of reading and writing. Special thanks to Nick Foley, the Salisbury Roaders, and 12-week warriors led by accountability champion Alison Jones.

Thank you to all the writing organisations we have worked with over the years, especially to Arvon and the ladies of Lumb. To all the writers we've workshopped, coached and cajoled to write. Supporting writers helped us make sense of what works in practice from the endless research on productivity, behaviour change and writing. To all readers and everyone who has an inkling of an idea to write – you can do it, you just need to start.

Finally, we'd like to give our ancient labradoodle Peggy a tickle on the scruff and a pig's ear to munch for being a writer's best friend over the years. While Peggy was light on editorial feedback, walks with her were transformative. If we hadn't left our desks to take a walk, this book wouldn't exist. Which gives us our very last opportunity to lever in a productivity tip – when you feel like you shouldn't take a break, *that's exactly when you should*.

REFERENCES

Epigraph

1. *Today*, BBC Radio 4, Jimmy McGovern interview, 15 July 2022 2 hours 44 minutes. https://www.bbc.co.uk/programmes/m00194bf

Introduction

1. Lucas, B.J., & Nordgren, L.F., 'People underestimate the value of persistence for creative performance', *Journal of Personality and Social Psychology*, 109(2), August 2015. https://www.scholars.northwestern.edu/en/publications/people-underestimate-the-value-of-persistence-for-creative-perfor

2. 'Falling short: seven writers reflect on failure', *Guardian*, 22 June 2013. https://www.theguardian.com/books/2013/jun/22/falling-short-writers-reflect-failure#Atwood

3. *Write*, Guardian Books, 2012

4. Maran, Meredith, *Why We Write*, Plume, 2013

5. Evans, B., Smith, C., & Tulley, C. 'The life of a productive scholarly author', 2019 https://prolifiko.com/wp-content/uploads/2019/03/Life-of-a-Productive-Scholar_-Key-Findings-Report.pdf

6. Kwok, Roberta, 'You can get that paper, thesis or grant written – with a little help', *Nature*, 30 March 2020. https://www.nature.com/articles/d41586-020-00917-5

7. Burkeman, Oliver, 'Is a daily routine all it's cracked up to be?', *Guardian*, 19 April 2019. https://www.theguardian.com/lifeandstyle/2019/apr/19/daily-routine-cracked-productive-regimen

8. Kamler, B., & Thomson, P. 'The failure of dissertation advice books: Toward alternative pedagogies for doctoral writing', *Educational Researcher*, 37(8), November 2008. https://doi.org/10.3102/0013189X08327390

Chapter 1

1. *The Tim Ferriss Show*, 'How to Be Creative Like a Motherf*cker – Cheryl Strayed. (#231)', 30 March 2017. https://tim.blog/2017/03/30/cheryl-strayed/

2. Ibid.

3. Sword, Helen, '"Write every day!": a mantra dismantled', *International Journal for Academic Development*, 21(4), 2016. https://www.tandfonline.com/doi/full/10.1080/1360144X.2016.1210153

4. Gourevitch, Philip (ed.), *The Paris Review Interviews*, vol. 4, Canongate Books, 2009

5. Maran, Meredith, *Why We Write*. Plume, 2013

6. Dore, Madeleine, 'Austin Kleon: A writer who draws', *Extraordinary Routines*. https://extraordinaryroutines.com/austin-kleon/

7. Maran, ibid.

8. Valby, Karen, 'Who is Elena Ferrante? An interview with the mysterious Italian author', *Entertainment Weekly*, 5 September 2014. https://ew.com/article/2014/09/05/elena-ferrante-italian-author-interview/

9. Currey, Mason, *Daily Rituals: Women at Work*, Picador, 2019

10. 'Bestselling Crime Writer Jeffery Deaver On 150-Page Outlines, Knowing What Readers Want, and Studying the Greats', *Writing Routines*. https://www.writingroutines.com/jeffery-deaver-interview/

11. Dweck Carol S., *Mindset*, Robinson, 2012

12. Ibid.

Chapter 2

1. Ashworth, Jenn, *Notes Made While Falling*, Goldsmiths Press, 2019

2. Boice, Robert, *Procrastination and Blocking: A Novel, Practical Approach*, Praegar, 1996

3. Darwin Correspondence Project, University of Cambridge. https://www.darwinproject.ac.uk/confessing-murder

4. Harper Lee in conversation with WQXR host Roy Newquist, 1964. https://www.youtube.com/watch?v=EfsFeMRF7CU

5. Nocera, Joe, 'The Harper Lee "Go Set a Watchman" Fraud', *New York Times*, 24 July 2015. https://www.nytimes.com/2015/07/25/opinion/joe-nocera-the-watchman-fraud.html

6. Cep, Casey, *Furious Hours: Murder, Fraud and the Last Trial of Harper Lee*, William Heinemann, 2019

7. Langer, Ellen J, *Mindfulness*, Da Capo Press, 1989

8. 'Mindfulness in the Age of Complexity', *Harvard Business Review*, March 2014. https://hbr.org/2014/03/mindfulness-in-the-age-of-complexity

9. 'Insanity Is Doing the Same Thing Over and Over Again and Expecting Different Results', Quote Investigator. https://quoteinvestigator.com/2017/03/23/same/

10. Heffernan, Margaret, *Uncharted: How Uncertainty Can Power Change*, Simon & Schuster, 2021

11. Evans, Bec, 'How to write a book in 100 days', Prolifiko, 4 September 2019. https://prolifiko.com/how-to-write-a-book-in-100-days/

12. 'Mindfulness in the Age of Complexity'. https://hbr.org/2014/03/mindfulness-in-the-age-of-complexity

Chapter 3

1. Allcott, Graham, 'Creativity and productivity', *Productive Mag*. http://productivemag.com/20/creativity-and-productivity

2. Evans, Bec, 'Get the Habit', *Mslexia*, 65, Mar/Apr/May 2015

3. The Extraordinary Business Book Club, 'Productivity and Focus with Graham Allcott', 18 April 2016. http://extraordinarybusinessbooks.com/ebbc-episode-5-productivity-and-focus-with-graham-allcott/

4. Newport, Cal, *Deep Work: Rules for Focused Success in a Distracted World*, Piatkus, 2016

5. Evans, Bec, 'How to make time to write – 4 approaches to finding time in busy schedules', 8 February 2021. https://prolifiko.com/make-time-to-write/

6. Allcott, Graham, *How to Be a Productivity Ninja: Worry Less, Achieve More and Love What You Do*, Icon Books, 2016

7. Tulley, Christine, *How Writing Faculty Write: Strategies for Process, Product, and Productivity*, Utah State University Press, 2018

8. Schulte, Brigid, 'Why time is a feminist issue', *Sydney Morning Herald*, 9 March 2015. https://www.smh.com.au/lifestyle/health-and-wellness/brigid-schulte-why-time-is-a-feminist-issue-20150309-13zimc.html

9. Whillans, Ashley. *Time Smart: How to Reclaim Your Time and Live a Happier Life*, Harvard Business Review Press, 2020

10. Evans, Bec, 'Finding time to write: the spontaneous writer', Prolifko, 24 October 2019. https://prolifiko.com/spontaneous-writing/

11. Smith, Chris, 'How writing scholars write: productivity tips from the best of the best', Prolifko, 1 May 2018. https://prolifiko.com/how-writing-scholars-write-productivity-tips-from-the-best-of-the-best/

12. Trollope, Anthony *An Autobiography* (Sadleir, M., and Page, F., eds), Oxford University Press, 1950 (reissued 1999)

13. Evans, Bec, 'Finding time to write: create a daily writing routine', Prolifko, 21 October 2019. https://prolifiko.com/find-time-to-write-daily/

14. Prolifiko, *The Life of a Productive Scholarly Author: How academics write, the barriers they face and why publishers and institutions should feel optimistic*, March 2019. https://prolifiko.com/wp-content/uploads/2019/03/Life-of-a-Productive-Scholar_-Key-Findings-Report.pdf

15. Trollope, ibid.

16. *The Tim Ferriss Show*, 'How to Be Creative Like a Motherf*cker—Cheryl Strayed (#231)'

17. Ibid.

18. Murray, Rowena, *Writing in Social Spaces: A Social Processes Approach to Academic Writing*, Routledge, 2015

19. Boice, Robert, 'Procrastination, busyness and bingeing', *Behaviour Research and Therapy*, 27(6), 1989, https://doi.org/10.1016/0005-7967(89)90144-7

20. Evans, Bec, 'Finding time to write: the deep worker', Prolifiko, 23 October 2019. https://prolifiko.com/deep-worker-writing/

21. Newport, Cal, 'Fixed-schedule productivity: How I accomplish a large amount of work in a small number of work hours', Study Hacks Blog, 15 February 2008. https://www.calnewport.com/blog/2008/02/15/fixed-schedule-productivity-how-i-accomplish-a-large-amount-of-work-in-a-small-number-of-work-hours/

22. Valian, Virginia, 'Solving a work problem' in *Scholarly Writing and Publishing: Issues, Problems, and Solutions* (ed. Fox, Mary Frank), Westview Press, 1985, pp. 99–110

23. Evans, Bec, 'Finding time to write: the time boxer', Prolifiko, 22 October 2019. https://prolifiko.com/time-boxer/

24. Vanderkam, Laura, *168 Hours: You Have More Time Than You Think*, Portfolio Penguin, 2010

25. https://shutupwrite.com/; https://www.focusmate.com/; https://writershour.com/

26. Cirillo, Francesco, 'The Pomodoro Technique'. https://francescocirillo.com/pages/pomodoro-technique

Chapter 4

1. Butler, Octavia E., 'Positive Obsession', *Bloodchild and Other Stories*, Seven Stories Press, 1996, reissued 2005

2. Butler, Octavia E., 'Afterword to Crossover', in *Bloodchild and Other Stories*

3. Eyal, Nir, *Indistractable: How to Control Your Attention and Choose Your Life*, Bloomsbury, 2019

4. Doidge, Norman, *The Brain That Changes Itself: Stories of Personal Triumph from the Frontiers of Brain Science*, Penguin, 2008

5. Peale, Norman Vincent, *The Power of Positive Thinking*, Prentice Hall, 1952

6. The Secret website: https://www.thesecret.tv/history-of-the-secret/

7. Jennings, Rebecca, 'Shut up, I'm manifesting!' *Vox*, 23 October 2020. https://www.vox.com/the-goods/21524975/manifesting-does-it-really-work-meme

8. Google Trends data: https://trends.google.com/trends/explore?q=manifesting

9. @tomdaley, Instagram Reel, 24 January 2021. https://www.instagram.com/reel/CKcBpSfHVeZ/?

10. Daley, Tom, YouTube channel, 'Visualisation is key!', 24 January 2021. https://youtu.be/LdwfN4tom1o

11. Amos, Georgina, & Chouinard, Philippe, 'Mirror neuron system activation differs in experienced golfers compared to controls watching videos of golf compared to novel sports depending on conceptual versus motor familiarity', *Journal of Vision*, 18(10), September 2018. https://jov.arvojournals.org/article.aspx?articleid=2699421

12. Bernardi, N.F., De Buglio, M., Trimarchi, P.D., Chielli, A., & Bricolo, E., 'Mental practice promotes motor anticipation: evidence from skilled music performance'. *Frontiers in Human Neuroscience*, 7, August 2013. https://doi.org/10.3389/fnhum.2013.00451; Iorio, C., Brattico, E., Munk Larsen, F., Vuust, P., & Bonetti, L., 'The effect of mental practice on music memorization', *Psychology of Music*, 50(1), 2022. https://doi.org/10.1177/0305735621995234

13. Mielke, S., & Comeau, G., 'Developing a literature-based glossary and taxonomy for the study of mental practice in music performance', *Musicae Scientiae*, 23(2), June 2019. https://doi.org/10.1177/1029864917715062

14. Driskell, J.E., Copper, C., & Moran, A., 'Does mental practice enhance performance?', *Journal of Applied Psychology*, 79(4), 1994. https://doi.org/10.1037/0021-9010.79.4.481

15. Open Culture, 'Behold Octavia Butler's Motivational Notes to Self', 29 June 2020. http://www.openculture.com/2020/06/behold-octavia-butlers-motivational-notes-to-self.html

16. Locke, E.A., Shaw, K.N., Saari, L.M., & Latham, G.P., 'Goal setting and task performance: 1969–1980', *Psychological Bulletin*, 90(1), 1981. https://doi.org/10.1037/0033-2909.90.1.125

17. Locke, Edwin A., & Latham, Gary P., *A Theory of Goal-Setting and Task Performance*, Prentice Hall, 1990

18. Evaristo, Bernardine, *Manifesto: On Never Giving Up*, Hamish Hamilton, 2021

19. Latham, G.P., Ganegoda, D.B., & Locke, E.A., 'Goal-setting: A state theory, but related to traits', in Chamorro-Premuzic, T., von Stumm, S., & Furnham, A. (eds), *The Wiley-Blackwell Handbook of Individual Differences*, Wiley Blackwell, 2011

20. Rhimes, Shonda, *Year of Yes*, Simon & Schuster, 2016

21. Holland, Cara, 'How to visualise your writing dreams and goals', Prolifiko, 19 December 2017. https://prolifiko.com/visualise-writing-dreams-goals/

22. Cameron, Julia, *The Artist's Way*, Pan Macmillan, 1995

23. Since interviewing her in 2018, Dr Gabija Toleikyte has written about this in her book with a more detailed exercise. Read: *Why the F*ck Can't I Change? Insights From a Neuroscientist to Show That You Can*, Thread, 2021

24. Check out www.futureme.org

Chapter 5

1. Evans, Bec, 'How small steps lead to great progress', 30 January 2020. https://prolifiko.com/small-steps/

2. Saad, Layla, F., 'I need to talk to spiritual white women about white supremacy (Part One)', 15 August 2017. http://laylafsaad.com/poetry-prose/white-women-white-supremacy-1

3. *Ctrl Alt Delete* podcast, 'Layla F Saad: Doing the anti-racism work', 4 June 2020. https://play.acast.com/s/ctrlaltdelete/-266laylasaad-doingtheanti-racismwork

4. Lao Tzu, *Tao Te Ching: A New English Version* (trans. Mitchell, S.), HarperPerennial, 1992, Chapter 63

5. Saad, ibid.

6. Maurer, Robert, *One Small Step Can Change Your Life: The Kaizen Way*, Workman Publishing, 2004

7. Fogg, B.J., *Tiny Habits: The Small Changes That Change Everything*, Penguin Random House, 2019

8. http://laylafsaad.com/meandwhitesupremacy

9. @laylafsaad, 'Today is the two year anniversary of the Me and White Supremacy Instagram challenge', 28 June 2020. https://www.instagram.com/p/CB-QxnEJbgl/

10. Saad, Layla, F., 'Leveling up: Welcome to my next (r)evolution', 7 August 2018. http://laylafsaad.com/poetry-prose/leveling-up

11. Lao Tzu, *Tao Te Ching: A New English Version* (trans. Mitchell, S.), HarperPerennial, 1992, Chapter 64

12. Fogg, ibid.

13. Leow, Rachel, @idlethink, 'just misread "24hr bookdrop" as "24hr bookshop". the disappointment is beyond words', 15 November 2008, https://twitter.com/idlethink/status/1006813155

14. Sloan, Robin, *Mr. Penumbra's 24-Hour Bookstore, the story*. https://www.robinsloan.com/books/penumbra/short-story/

15. Kickstarter, 'Robin writes a book (and you get a copy)'. https://www.kickstarter.com/projects/robinsloan/robin-writes-a-book-and-you-get-a-copy

16. Sloan, Robin, 'Penumbra has a posse', https://www.robinsloan.com/notes/penumbra-posse/

17. Nickels, Colin, & Davis, Hilary, 'Understanding researcher needs and raising the profile of library research support', *Insights* 33(1), 2020. http://doi.org/10.1629/uksg.493

18. Lodge, David, *Consciousness & the Novel: Connected Essays*, Harvard University Press, 2004

19. Alter, Alexandra, 'EL James interview: "There are other stories I want to tell. I've been with Fifty Shades for so long"', 17 April 2019. https://www.independent.co.uk/arts-entertainment/books/fatures/el-james-fifty-shade-grey-mister-new-novel-a8873216.html

20. Bandura, A., & Schunk, D.H., 'Cultivating competence, self-efficacy, and intrinsic interest through proximal self-motivation', *Journal of Personality and Social Psychology*, 41(3), 1981. http://dx.doi.org/10.1037/0022-3514.41.3.586

21. Fogg, ibid.

22. Sloan, Robin, 'Writing and lightness', March 2020. https://www.robinsloan.com/notes/writing-and-lightness/

23. Jung R.E., Wertz, C.J., Meadows, C.A., Ryman, S.G., Vakhtin, A.A., & Flores, R.A., 'Quantity yields quality when it comes to creativity: a brain and behavioral test of the equal-odds rule', *Frontiers in Psychology*, 6, article 864, 25 June 2015. https://doi.org/10.3389/fpsyg.2015.00864

Chapter 6

1. Gaiman, Neil, 'Entitlement issues...' *Journal*, 12 May 2009. https://journal.neilgaiman.com/2009/05/entitlement-issues.html

2. Renfro, Kim, 'George R.R. Martin's friends explain the complicated reasons his next book might be taking so long to write', *Insider*, 25 April 2018. https://www.insider.com/why-winds-of-winter-is-taking-so-long-2017-1

3. '"Winds of Winter" release date: George R.R. Martin explains why it's taking so long to complete book: "Writer's block isn't to blame"', *HNGN*, 22 October 2014. https://www.hngn.com/articles/46711/20141022/winds-of-winter-release-date-george-r-r-martin-explains-why-its-taking-so-long-to-complete-book-writers-block-isnt-to-blame.htm

4. Martin, George R.R., 'Back in Westeros', *Not a Blog*. 15 August 2020. https://georgerrmartin.com/notablog/2020/08/15/back-in-westeros/

5. Kahneman, Daniel, *Thinking, Fast and Slow*, Penguin, 2012

6. Ibid.

7. Ibid.

8. Carr, Nicholas, *The Shallows: What the Internet Is Doing to Our Brains*, Atlantic Books, 2010

9. Gallagher, Winifred, *Rapt: Attention and the Focused Life*, Penguin, 2009

10. Zhu, Erping, 'Hypermedia interface design: the effects of number of links and granularity of nodes', *Journal of Educational Multimedia and Hypermedia*, 8(3), 1999. https://eric.ed.gov/?id=EJ603768

11. Dolan, Paul, *Happiness by Design: Finding Pleasure and Purpose in Everyday Life*, Penguin, 2014

12. 'Interview Larry King with Gabriele Oettingen', 26 March 2020. https://www.youtube.com/watch?v=6TfO2fNW_ZU

13. Oettingen, Gabriele, *Rethinking Positive Thinking: Inside the New Science of Motivation*, Penguin, 2015

14. Ibid.

15. Elliot, Jeffrey, M., *Conversations with Maya Angelou*, University Press of Mississippi, 1989

16. Gourevitch, Philip (ed.), *The Paris Review Interviews*, vol. 4, Canongate, 2009

17. 'Maya Angelou with George Plimpton: 92NY/The Paris Review Interview Series'. https://www.youtube.com/watch?v=XYn3HFg_T0o&t=18s

18. Cialdini, Robert, *Pre-suasion: A Revolutionary Way to Influence and Persuade*, Random House, 2016

19. Ibid.

20. Hemingway, Ernest, 'Monologue to the maestro: A high seas letter', *Esquire*, 1 October 1935. https://classic.esquire.com/article/1935/10/1/monologue-to-the-maestro

21. Evans, Bec, 'Oliver Burkeman's ten top tips for a productive and happy writing life', Prolifko, 28 November 2014. https://prolifiko.com/oliver-burkemans-top-ten-tips-for-a-productive-and-happy-writing-life/

Chapter 7

1. Gittings, G., Bergman, M., Shuck, B. and Rose, K. 'The impact of student attributes and program characteristics on doctoral degree completion', *New Horizons in Adult Education and Human Resource Development*, 30(3), 2018. https://doi.org/10.1002/nha3.20220

2. Lindner, Rebecca, *Barriers to Doctoral Education: Equality, Diversity and Inclusion for Postgraduate Research Students at UCL*, UCL Doctoral School, July 2020. https://www.grad.ucl.ac.uk/strategy/barriers-to-doctoral-education.pdf

3. Masten, Ann S., *Ordinary Magic: Resilience in Development*, Guilford Press, 2014

4. American Psychological Association, 'Building your resilience', 1 January 2012. https://www.apa.org/topics/resilience/building-your-resilience

5. 'Interview Larry King with Gabriele Oettingen', ibid.

6. WOOP Toolkit, https://woopmylife.org/en/home

References

Chapter 8

1. Pink, Daniel H., *The Power of Regret: How Looking Backwards Moves us Forward*, Canongate, 2022

2. Doney, P., Evans, R., & Fabri, M., 'Keeping creative writing on track: Co-designing a framework to support behaviour change', in Marcus, A. (ed.), *Design, User Experience, and Usability. Theories, Methods, and Tools for Designing the User Experience, Lecture Notes in Computer Science*, 8517, 2014. https://doi.org/10.1007/978-3-319-07668-3_61

3. Chapter XVIII: 'How we should struggle against appearances', from Book 2 of Arrian's *Discourses of Epictetus* (ed. Long, George). http://www.perseus.tufts.edu/hopper/text?doc=urn:cts:greekLit:tlg0557.tlg001.perseus-eng1:2.18

4. Harvard University, Department of Psychology, 'William James'. https://psychology.fas.harvard.edu/people/william-james

5. James, William, *The Principles of Psychology*, vol. 1, Henry Holt & Company, 1918

6. Andrews, B.R., 'Habit', *American Journal of Psychology*, 14(2), April 1903. https://doi.org/10.2307/1412711

7. Barnett, Michaela, 'Good habits, bad habits: a conversation with Wendy Wood', *Behavioral Scientist*, 14 October 2019. https://behavioralscientist.org/good-habits-bad-habits-a-conversation-with-wendy-wood/

8. The Booker Prize, 'The Man (Booker) in a Van', 5 August 2016

9. Duncan, P., Ulmanu, M., & Louter, D., 'How to finish a novel: Tracking a book's progress from idea to completion', *Guardian*, 20 March 2017. https://www.theguardian.com/books/ng-interactive/2017/mar/20/how-to-finish-a-novel-tracking-book-progress-wyl-menmuir

10. Landay, William, 'How writers write: Graham Greene', 8 July 2009. https://www.williamlanday.com/2009/07/08/how-writers-write-graham-greene/

11. *Freakonomics* podcast, 'Here's why all your projects are always late – and what to do about it', episode 323, 7 March 2018. https://freakonomics.com/podcast/heres-why-all-your-projects-are-always-late-and-what-to-do-about-it/

12. Menmuir, Wyl, 'Why I track and monitor my writing progress', Prolifko, 8 September 2017. https://prolifiko.com/benefits_of_tracking_your_writing/

13. Norcross J.C., & Vangarelli D.J., 'The resolution solution: longitudinal examination of New Year's change attempts', *Journal of Substance Abuse*, 1(2), 1988–9, pp. 127–34. https://doi.org/10.1016/S0899-3289(88)80016-6

14. Wood, Wendy, *Good Habits, Bad Habits: The Science of Making Positive Changes That Stick*, Pan Macmillan, 2021

15. Ibid.

16. Duhigg, Charles, *The Power of Habit: Why We Do What We Do and How to Change*, Penguin Random House, 2013

17. Steinbeck, John, *Working Days: The Journals of The Grapes of Wrath*, Penguin, 2019

18. Wood, ibid.

19. Ward, A.F., Duke, K., Gneezy, A., & Bos, M.W., 'Brain drain: The mere presence of one's own smartphone reduces available cognitive capacity', *Journal of the Association for Consumer Research*, 2(2), April 2017. https://www.journals.uchicago.edu/doi/10.1086/691462

20. Lally, P., van Jaarsveld, C.H.M., Potts, H.W.W., & Wardle, J., 'How habits are formed: Modelling habit formation in the real world', *European Journal of Social Psychology*, 40(6), October 2010. https://doi.org/10.1002/ejsp.674

21. Wood, ibid.

22. Fogg, ibid.

23. Dictionary.com, 'Incentive'. https://www.dictionary.com/browse/incentive

24. Rubin, Gretchen, *Better Than Before: What I Learned About Making and Breaking Habits – to Sleep More, Quit Sugar, Procrastinate Less, and Generally Build a Happier Life*, Two Roads, 2015

25. *In Writing with Hattie Crisell* podcast, 'Meg Mason, novelist', series 4, episode 37, 5 November 2021. https://audioboom.com/posts/7974168-meg-mason-novelist

26. Trapani, Gina, 'Jerry Seinfeld's productivity secret', *Lifehacker*, 24 July 2007. https://lifehacker.com/jerry-seinfelds-productivity-secret-281626

27. Duhigg, ibid.

28. Chonotype: Automated Morningness-Eveningness Questionnaire (AutoMEQ): https://chronotype-self-test.info/

29. Fogg, ibid.

30. Currey, Mason, *Daily Rituals: How Great Minds Make Time, Find Inspiration, and Get to Work*, Picador, 2013

31. Austin Kleon has a brilliant 100-day wall chart you can print off from his website. https://www.dropbox.com/s/16are47xphabayb/practice-suck-less-100-days.pdf?dl=0

Chapter 9

1. McGrail, M.R., Rickard, C.M., & Jones, R.M., 'Publish or perish: A systematic review of interventions to increase academic publication rates', *Research & Development*, 25(1), 2006

2. Duhigg, , ibid.

References

3. Dowling, David, O., *A Delicate Aggression: Savagery and Survival in the Iowa Writers' Workshop*, Yale University Press, 2019

4. Doherty, Maggie, 'Unfinished work: How sexism and machismo shapes a prestigious writing program', *New Republic*, 24 April 2019. https://newrepublic.com/article/153487/sexism-machismo-iowa-writers-workshop

5. Ibid.

6. *Trust Me, I'm a Doctor*, 'The big motivation experiment', BBC2. https://www.bbc.co.uk/programmes/articles/3hRfJqQDPLW5ZbqQCQS1K1v/the-big-motivation-experiment

7. McConnachie, James, 'Emerging from lockdown', *The Author*, summer 2020. https://societyofauthors.org/News/The-Author/Summer-2020

8. Walton, G.M., Cohen, G.L., Cwir, D., & Spencer, S.J., 'Mere belonging: The power of social connections', *Journal of Personality and Social Psychology*, 102(3), 2012. https://doi.org/10.1037/a0025731

9. Murphy Paul, Annie, *The Extended Mind: The Power of Thinking Outside the Brain*, Houghton Mifflin Harcourt, 2021

10. Cornwell, Nick, 'My father was famous as John le Carré. My mother was his crucial, covert collaborator', *Guardian*, 13 March 2021. https://www.theguardian.com/books/2021/mar/13/my-father-was-famous-as-john-le-carre-my-mother-was-his-crucial-covert-collaborator

11. Daniell, Tina, & McGilligan, Pat, 'Betty Comden and Adolph Green: Almost improvisation', in McGilligan, Patrick (ed.), *Backstory 2: Interviews with Screenwriters of the 1940s and 1950s*, University of California Press, 1991. http://ark.cdlib.org/ark:/13030/ft0z09n7m0/

12. Rubin, Gretchen, *The Four Tendencies: The Indispensable Personality Profiles That Reveal How to Make Your Life Better (and Other People's Lives, Too)*, Two Roads, 2017

13. The Four Tendencies Quiz: https://quiz.gretchenrubin.com/

14. Sword, Helen, *Air & Light & Time & Space: How Successful Academics Write*, Harvard University Press, 2017

15. Rees, Jasper, *Let's Do It, The Authorised Biography of Victoria Wood*, Trapeze, 2020

16. Jeffries, Stuart, 'Victoria Wood obituary', *Guardian*, 20 April 2016. https://www.theguardian.com/culture/2016/apr/20/victoria-wood-obituary

17. https://www.bafta.org/heritage/in-memory-of/victoria-wood, https://www.royalalberthall.com/about-the-hall/news/2016/april/remembering-victoria-wood-the-royal-albert-halls-record-breaking-comedian/

18. Levittt, Steven D., 'Gary Becker, 1930–2014', *Freakonomics*, 5 May 2014. https://freakonomics.com/2014/05/gary-becker-1930-2014/

Written

19. Matthews, Gail, 'The impact of commitment, accountability, and written goals on goal achievement', *Psychology: Faculty Presentations*, 3, 2007. https://scholar.dominican.edu/psychology-faculty-conference-presentations/3

Chapter 10

1. Oates, Joyce Carol, 'The Magnanimity of Wuthering Heights', *Critical Inquiry*, winter 1983

2. Oates, Joyce Carol, quoted in Plimpton, G. (ed.), *Women Writers at Work: The Paris Review Interviews*, Penquin Press, 1989

3. US Department of Education, 'Typical language accomplishments for children, birth to age 6 – Helping your child become a reader'. https://www2.ed.gov/parents/academic/help/reader/part9.html

4. Kellogg, Ronald T., 'Training writing skills: A cognitive development perspective', *Journal of Writing Research*, 1(1), 2008

5. The British Library, 'Earliest known writings of Charlotte Brontë'. https://www.bl.uk/collection-items/earliest-known-writings-of-charlotte-bronte

6. Kellogg, ibid.

7. Friar, Nicola, 'The importance of the child author', 17 July 2017. https://brontebabeblog.wordpress.com/2017/07/17/first-blog-post/

8. Friar, Nicola, 'Autobiography, wish-fulfilment, and juvenilia: The "fractured self" in Charlotte Brontë's paracosmic counterworld', *Journal of Juvenilia Studies*, 2(2), 2019. https://journalofjuveniliastudies.com/index.php/jjs/article/view/21/39

9. Ericsson, Anders, & Pool, Robert, *Peak: Secrets from the New Science of Expertise*, Penguin Random House, 2016

10. Chase, W.G., & Simon, H.A., 'Perception in chess', *Cognitive Psychology*, 4(1), 1973. https://doi.org/10.1016/0010-0285(73)90004-2

11. Ericsson, K.A., Krampe, R.T., & Tesch-Römer, C., 'The role of deliberate practice in the acquisition of expert performance', *Psychological Review*, 100(3), 1993. https://doi.org/10.1037/0033-295X.100.3.363

12. 'Interview: Paul McCartney heads to Canada', *CBC*, 6 August 2010. https://www.cbc.ca/news/entertainment/interview-paul-mccartney-heads-to-canada-1.942764

13. Ericsson & Pool, ibid.

14. Ericsson, K.A., Prietula, M.J., Cokely, E.T., 'The making of an expert', *Harvard Business Review*, July–August 2007. https://hbr.org/2007/07/the-making-of-an-expert

15. Ibid.

16. Ericsson, K.A., 'Commentaries: Creative expertise and superior reproducible performance: Innovative and flexible aspects of expert performance', *Psychological Inquiry*, 10(3). https://doi.org/10.1207/S15327965PLI1004_5

17. Ericsson, Prietula & Cokely, ibid.

18. Ericsson, Prietula & Cokely, ibid.

19. Franklin, Benjamin, *Autobiography of Benjamin Franklin* (ed. Woodworth Pine, Frank), Henry Holt and Company, 1916

20. Ericsson & Pool, ibid.

21. Ibid.

22. Ong, Walter J., *An Ong Reader: Challenges for Further Inquiry*, Hampton Press Communication, 2002

23. Sommers, Nancy, 'Revision strategies of student writers and experienced adult writers', *College Composition and Communication*, 31(4), December 1980. https://doi.org/10.2307/356588

24. Ericsson & Pool, ibid.

25. Ibid.

26. Ericsson, K.A., Krampe, R.T., & Tesch-Römer, C., 'The role of deliberate practice in the acquisition of expert performance', *Psychological Review*, 100(3), 1993. https://doi.org/10.1037/0033-295X.100.3.363 quoting Cowley, M. (ed.), *Writers at Work: The Paris Review Interviews*, Viking Press, 1959 and Plimpton, G. (ed.), *Writers at Work: The Paris Review Interviews*, Penguin Books, 1977

27. Colvin, Geoff, *Talent Is Overrated: What Really Separates World-Class Performers from Everyone Else*, Nicholas Brealey, 2008

Conclusion

1. Simonton, D.K., 'Creative productivity, age, and stress: A biographical time-series analysis of 10 classical composers', *Journal of Personality and Social Psychology*, 35(11), 1977. https://doi.org/10.1037/0022-3514.35.11.791

2. Simonton, D.K., 'Thomas Edison's creative career: The multi-layered trajectory of trials, errors, failures and triumphs', *Psychology of Aesthetics, Creativity and the Arts*, 9(1), 2015. https://doi.org/10.1037/a0037722

3. Simonton, D.K., 'Creative productivity: A predictive and explanatory model of career trajectories and landmarks', *Psychological Review*, 104(1), 1997. https://citeseerx.ist.psu.edu/viewdoc/download?doi=10.1.1.391.5108&rep=rep1&type=pdf

4. Grant, Adam, *Originals: How Non-Conformists Move the World*, Viking, 2016

5. Simonton, ibid.

6. Smith, Chris, 'The surprising creative hobbies of superstar scholars – and what you can learn', 24 April 2018. https://prolifiko.com/surprsing-creative-hobbies-of-superstar-scholar/

7. Lucas & Nordgren, 'People underestimate the value of persistence for creative performance'

8. Townsend, Sue, 'Book Club: The Secret Diary of Adrian Mole, Aged 13¾ by Sue Townsend', *Guardian*, 18 December 2010. https://www.theguardian.com/books/2010/dec/18/adrian-mole-sue-townsend-bookclub

9. *Longform*, podcast, '#376: Kevin Kelly', January 2020. https://longform.org/posts/longform-podcast-376-kevin-kelly

PERMISSIONS

This book was brought to you through the team
effort of the following people at Icon Books
and our wonderful freelancers.

Editorial
Duncan Heath
Kiera Jamison

Sales
Andrew Furlow
Matt Boxell
Annalise Peters

Marketing and Publicity
Emily Cary-Elwes
Hamza Jahanzeb
Temi Gadu

Typesetting and Internal Design
Marie Doherty

Cover Design
Dan Mogford

Production
Thea Hirsi

Accounts
Chanelle McKenzie

Copy Editor
Hanna Milner

Proofreader
Alice Brett